Thomas Jefferys

Voyages from Asia to America,

for Completing the Discoveries of the North West Coast of America

Thomas Jefferys

Voyages from Asia to America,
for Completing the Discoveries of the North West Coast of America

ISBN/EAN: 9783744793674

Printed in Europe, USA, Canada, Australia, Japan

Cover: Foto ©Andreas Hilbeck / pixelio.de

More available books at **www.hansebooks.com**

VOYAGES
FROM
ASIA to AMERICA,
For Completing the DISCOVERIES of the
North West Coast of *America*.
To which is prefixed,

A SUMMARY of the VOYAGES
Made by the *RUSSIANS* on the
FROZEN SEA,
In SEARCH of a NORTH EAST Paſſage.

Serving as an Explanation of a Map of the Ruſſian *Diſcoveries, publiſhed by the Academy of Sciences at* Peterſburgh.

Tranſlated from the *High Dutch* of
S. MULLER, of the Royal Academy of *Peterſburgh*.

WITH THE ADDITION OF THREE NEW MAPS;

1. A Copy of Part of the *Japaneſe* Map of the World.
2. A Copy of *De Liſle*'s and *Buache*'s fictitious Map. And
3. A large Map of *Canada*, extending to the *Pacific Ocean*, containing the New *Diſcoveries* made by the RUSSIANS and FRENCH.

By THOMAS JEFFERYS Geographer to his Majeſty.

LONDON:
Printed for T. JEFFERYS, the Corner of *St. Martin's-Lane, Charing Croſs*, 1761.

Land which
is supposed
to be the
FOU-SANG
of the
Chinese Geographers.

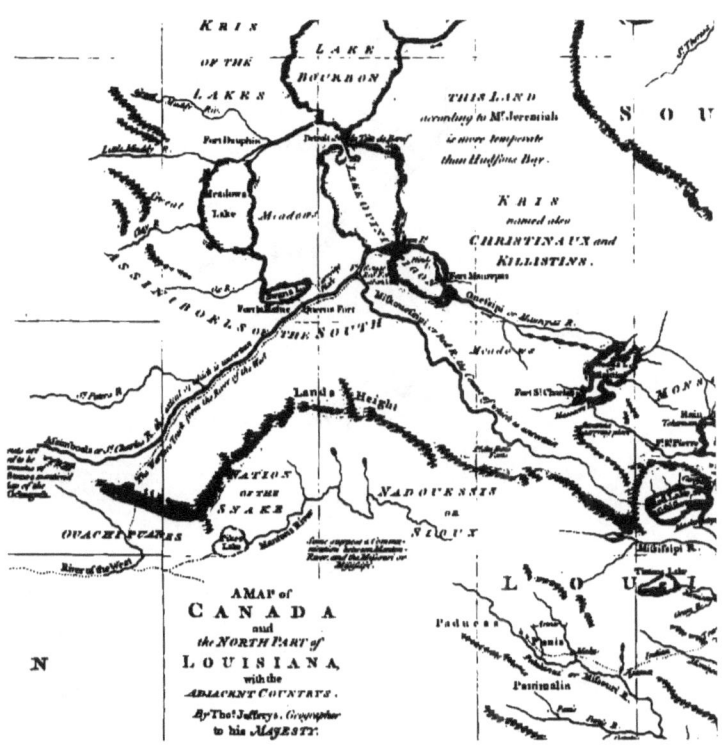

THE
EDITOR'S PREFACE.

TO ascertain the following Particulars hath been long Matter of eager Enquiry, equally among the curious and commercial Part of mankind, whether there is a Possibility of reaching the *East-Indies* by a shorter Way than that of doubling the *Cape* of *Good-Hope*; and whether the two great Continents of *Asia* and *America*, do actually any where join or not. In regard to the first Article, there are at present only two known Maritime Tracts, by which we have a free Communication with the *East-Indian* Part of the Globe, either round the Southernmost Promontory of *Africa*, to the Eastward, or that still more Southernly one of *America*, called *Cape-Horn*, to the Westward. The former of these, is almost wholly used by the several Nations of *Europe*, whose Commerce invites them to the *Indian Seas*, as being by much the shorter of the two, though yet the longest and most tedious of all usual Navigation. Various have been the Methods thought upon to facilitate our Arrival in these Parts, to shorten the vast Circuit taken about, and to save both the Time and Trouble expended in coasting round the Continent of *Africa*. As a Remedy against this Inconvenience, it has been projected to cut a Canal through the Neck of Land, intercepted between the most Northern Extent of the *Red Sea*, and the opposite Part of the *Levant*, (which dividing *Asia*

(iv)

from *Africa*, renders the latter a great Peninsula,) and so to make an uninterrupted Passage to the *Indian Sea*, from the *Mediterranean* through the *Straits* of *Babelmandel*; but this Scheme, though concerted and begun to be put in Execution, more than once, in remote Ages, was found to be impracticable, and the Projectors were obliged to desist, after having consumed Multitudes of Men in the Attempt, either from the Difficulty of cutting through vast Mountains and Beds of Granate in the Way, or a Fear of what Consequences might ensue from a Junction of those Seas; the *Red Sea* being naturally supposed to be much higher than the *Mediterranean*; because the *Nile* empties itself into the latter; the Event, therefore, of a Junction of such vast Bodies of Water, they dreaded might cause great Devastation by the over-filling of the *Mediterranean*, which in all Probability would have laid *Egypt* entirely under Water. Besides, as the *Turks* govern the Country on both Sides the *Red Sea*, they would also be Masters of the Passage, and levy what exorbitant Tax they should think proper to demand, in Opposition to all the Powers in *Europe*, though they united in fighting for this Door to the *East-Indies*.

Another Project was, that of cutting a Way for sailing from *Europe* to *Asia*, through the narrowest Part of the *Streights* of *Darien*; a Neck of Land, which connects the two Continents of Northern and Southern *America* together; but the Execution of this Design must meet with insurmountable Obstacles, from a Want of Numbers sufficient to accomplish so vast an Enterprize, as well as Provisions to subsist them during their Labours, was it possible to bring thither an adequate Number of hands; not to mention that the Unhealthiness of the Climate, and the Fatigue joined with it, would be so destructive to the People employed, that perhaps the whole Maritime Power of *Europe* would be scarcely able to furnish out Men requisite for this Purpose, and supply the continual Waste of human Lives.

These Schemes being therefore justly deemed visionary, and impracticable, Men cast about to find whether Nature had offered to them any other Method of rendering the Voyage to the *East-Indies* less tedious and irksome. Two Ways only now presented themselves to be tried, the one to the North West round *America*, the other to the North East, about the most Northernly Coasts of *Europe* and *Asia*. Both have been attempted without Success hitherto, though the following Treatise makes it plain to Demonstration, that there is, throughout the latter mentioned Voyage, a Continuation of Sea extending to *China* and *Japan*. Indeed, if we consider the extreme

Dif-

Difficulties that would occur in a North-West Voyage by the Coast of *America*, that round *Europe* and the Northern Boundary of *Asia*, into the *Indian Seas*, is the most feasible; and what Hopes there are of its future Success, the following Work will demonstrate, which is divided into two Parts. The First contains an Account of the several Journies, Voyages, and Expeditions, which were made to discover the Easternmost Extremity of *Asia*, and to determine whether the *Frozen Sea* was continued round from the most Northern Shores of *Europe*, along that of *Asia*, as far as to *Japan*; for they knew if so, the last mentioned Continent, and that of *America*, must be separated. By these Means also the Boundaries of the vast Empire of *Russia*, to the North and East, were fixed, and many of the scattered and barbarous Nations that inhabit those prodigious Tracts of Land, reduced under some Sort of Regulation. The Second Part relates the Voyages and Adventures of the Commanders and Mariners, that by the Order of the late Czar, *Peter the Great*, and the succeeding Empress, were undertaken in order to prove whether *Asia* and *America* were any where connected; if not, how wide the Distance might be between them. These several Voyages, like all others that are made for the Discovery of unknown Coasts, were attended with great Perils and Distresses to the Navigators; but by their Assistance our Curiosity is at length satisfied, and we are certain of these two Points, from Proofs founded upon very authentic Testimonies, both that the Possibility of a North Eastern Passage to *India* does indeed exist, and that the abovementioned Continents are really separated by Sea from each other. But as in all Probability the Distance between the Extremities of each is not great, the Population of *America*, which has so long puzzled the Inquisitive, may be very fairly hence accounted for, since Accident might more than once have driven some of the Inhabitants of *Kamtchatka*, or *Ochotzk*, in their Boats too far out to Sea, for them to recover their native Shore, and have landed them upon the opposite Coast of *America*. Neither is it impossible, that the intermediate Channel in this severe Climate, may some Years be so entirely frozen over, at least for a time, as to have given those People an Opportunity of passing it on foot, whose Return back again a sudden Thaw of the Ice may naturally be supposed to have prevented. The Difference of Language, Customs, Shape, and Features, that appear between the *American* Savages and the Nations abovementioned, may arise from various Causes in the Course of so long a Tract of Time as may have passed since such a Chance as this first happened;

during

during which the same, most likely, hath been repeated often in distant Ages of the World.

But to return; I observed above, that there is indisputably, according to these Memoirs, a Passage along the Northern Coast of *Asia* round the *Tchutsebi Noss*, and so to the South by *Japan* into the *Indian Seas*, which is without Doubt a much nearer Way, meerly in regard to Distance, than the present Tract about the Cape of *Good Hope*. yet there is one grand Obstacle that, I am afraid, can never be so far overcome as to make the Voyage this Way practicable, even although the Course was much shorter than it is; I mean the vast Shoals of Ice, sometimes fixed and sometimes floating, that incessantly present themselves in the *Frozen Ocean*, which oftentimes congeal together in such a Manner as to form a new Continent, as it were, and freeze the Ships, that are unfortunate enough to be surrounded by them, fast for several Weeks together. The Delay, occasioned by this Circumstance, to the *Russian* Vessels, has been so great, that two or three Years have elapsed in making the Voyage from the *Lena* to *Kamtchatka*; it being hardly possible, during the short Extent of the Summer in these Parts, to pass through the broken Shoals of Ice before the Winter sets in again. And though undoubtedly the *British* Sailors are the most intrepid and skilful on the Globe, yet, provided the Voyage one Time with another should only take up Twelve Months from *Europe* to *India*, notwithstanding the vast Addition made to it is by the Circuit from *England* round *Norway*, *Lapland*, &c. into the *Frozen Ocean*, still this would be much more inconvenient, as well as of longer Duration, than the usual Tract about the Cape of *Good Hope*. The Danger and Misery that accrues, when a Stay is made of any Length of Time in such Climates, and the People are not continually exercised with Labour, is almost as intolerable as any Thing else, it inconceivable, I mean from that dreadful Distemper the Scurvy, which is always found in such Cases to make horrible ravages in the human Frame. Indeed it is very uncertain whether this Disorder could be prevented by any Means whatever, while the Men are forced to subsist upon Salt Provisions; and to supply them with Fresh in those Regions would be impossible; so that, upon the whole, such a Voyage seems, in my Opinion, altogether unfit and impossible to be executed with any tolerable Degree of Success, that can be depended upon, for facilitating a Communication between Nations so very remote from each other. It has been asserted that the Ocean under the Northern Pole is open, and but little incumbered with Ice, and that therefore

(vii)

therefore the Performance of the Voyage we are treating of, seems probable to be effected this Way; one would be loth to discourage any Endeavour to promote the public Benefit, but yet it should be considered, that was the Certainty of this Fact proved by repeated Testimonies, which is far from being the Case, even then the great Obstruction, both in entering and leaving the Polar Ocean, would still make the Voyage exceedingly hazardous, tedious, and uncertain. I have thought proper to make these few Animadversions upon the North-eastern Navigations, and shall now proceed to say something relating to the Work in general.

The Reader will here find, in their Order, the several Expeditions undertaken by the *Russians* and *Cossacks* to make themselves acquainted with some of the barbarous Nations, that roam over the vast Tract of *Northern Asia*, to extend the Limits of the *Muscovitish* Territories, and levy a Tribute from the Inhabitants of the only riches those Countries are as yet productive, of which are indeed the most properly suited to them, the warm and beautiful Furs wherewith Nature has cloathed many of the animals that are bred there. In the Course of these Narrations is a Number of curious and strange Particulars, which arise sometimes from the uncouth Customs, as they appear to us, of the rude Possessors; at others, from a Soil and Climate so different and distant from our own, that it is only from the *Russians* and *Cossacks* we can expect any authentic Information in what appertains to these rugged Regions, because they are not only better fitted to travel therein, and nearer of a Complexion in Temper and Disposition with the wild Nations that people them, but their Interest also, and the Gain they expect to make by Discoveries of this Sort, prompts them thus to exert themselves. The Reader will find the Stile of this Recital to be very unaffected and simple, being only a plain Translation of Memoirs of Voyages collected from the Original Manuscripts, containing the Discoveries made, Step by Step, along the Coasts of the *Frozen Sea*, and to the Continent of *America*, from the Year 1636 to that of 1742. In regard to the Maps, which are inserted for the better Explanation of the Matters related in the Work, the original Map of the *Russian* Discoveries, comprehending the Coast of *Asia*, from *Nova Zembla* round the *Tchutkschi* to the Isle of *Japan*, with the Course of the *Russia* Ships which actually sailed from the River *Lena* round the *Tchutski Noss* to *Kamtchatka*, and also the Tracts of Captain *Bering* and *Tchirekow*, from the Port of *Awatscha*, in *Kamtchatka*, likewise to the opposite Coasts of *North America*; I

have

(viii)

have likewife inferted on it the Routs of the feveral Travellers by Land and Sea, which are not in the Original; and added three other Maps.

The *Firft* is a Copy of Part of a *Japanefe* Map of the World, formerly belonging to Sir *Hans Sloane*'s Collection, now in the *Britifh Mufeum*, of the fame Parts of the Globe, which agree, in moft effential Particulars, with the *Ruffian* Accounts here given.

The *Second* is a Map copied according to the Forgeries and pretended Difcoveries collected by Meffrs. *De Lifle* and *Buache*.

The *Third* is a Map of *Canada* in *North America*, extending from Captain *Bering*'s Difcoveries in about 59 Degrees of North Latitude to 40 Southward, and thence in a Parallel as far as *Newfoundland*, laid down according to the moft accurate Obfervations, by which may be perceived the great Extent the *French* gave to *Canada*, even into the very remote Parts of this vaft Continent. What End they could purpofe to themfelves by publifhing fuch Falfities, in regard to the Form and Situation of Part of the Globe, is not eafy to determine, unlefs by a Pretence of having firft difcovered the whole, they intended to lay Claim to all the Eaftern, as well as to drive out and exclude us from all the Weftern Shores of the Northern Parts of the *New World*; if fo, we have now the Pleafure to fee their Artifices meeting a proper Retaliation from an injured Nation, and, inftead of gaining by their Encroachments upon others, they have loft all their valuable Settlements, and muft in the End, if we preferve what has been gallantly, as well as juftly purchafed by our Swords, be totally fubjugated in *North America*.

VOYAGES

A SUMMARY of

VOYAGES

Made by the *RUSSIANS* on the

F R O Z E N   S E A,

In Search of a

NORTH-EAST PASSAGE.

WHETHER *Asia* extends on the North East to *America*, has ever been an important Question amongst the Geographers. To obtain more certain Accounts of this, most European Nations were too remote. The Navigation must be made, either thro' the Frozen Sea, or the Southern Ocean; and upon this latter, either round about from the *East Indies*, or by the Way of *America*: We have nothing from the Voyages of the *English* and *Dutch* on the Frozen Sea, beyond *Nova Zembla*, that deserves Credit. The *Dutch* Discoveries in 1643, merely regard the Islands situated North East of *Japan*. The Landing of Sir *Francis Drake* on the *American* Coast, in the Year 1579, when he gave the Name of *New Albion* to a Tract of Land North of *California*, and the Voyage of *Martin d' Aguilar*, in the Year 1603, which was only a little farther to the North West, are the

a only

(ii)

only Attempts on the *American* Side, of which we have any certain Accounts. As to *John de Fuca*'s pretended Voyage, in the Year 1592, there are well-grounded Reasons to agree with those, who think it fictitious; and in the same Light, we may surely look upon all the Voyage of the *Spanish* Admiral *De Fonte*, in the Year 1640, till the Objections that have been raised against it are answered.

The Honour of doing something more, was reserved for the *Russian* Empire, which was much better situated for it; since its Limits extend to the same unknown and undiscovered Regions. The immortal Emperor *Peter* the Great, during his Residence in *Holland* in 1717, was requested to interest himself in this Affair, by those who were fond of new Discoveries. He drew up Orders with his own Hand, and delivered them to the Admiral in Chief, Count *Fedor Apraxin*.

At that Time it was not known at the Imperial Court, nor even in the remotest Part of *Siberia*, what had been done, and discovered above seventy Years before, by Voyages from *Jakutzk* * to the North Eastward of the Regions of *Siberia*. The North Easterly Isthmus of *Siberia*, commonly called *Tschukotzkoi Noss*, had been sailed round long before the *Russians* had reached as far as ‡ *Kamtschatka*, by this Navigation.

It

---

* *Jakutzk*, are a Pagan People, called so by the *Russians*; they are under the *Russian* Government, and live along the River *Lena*, and about the City of *Jakutski*; but they call themselves in their own Tongue, *Zinzacha*, or *Zinzogotock*. This is one of the most numerous Pagan Nations in *Siberia*, and consists of the following Tribes. 1. *Boro-Ganiska*. 2. *Bailungski*. 3. *Batly's*. 4. *Jock-Soyon*. 5. *Menga*. 6. *Kangalas*. 7. *Natmin*. 8. *Batbruski*. 9. *Lugai*. 10. *Belugur*. All which together, make about 30,000 Men who pay Scot and Lot. They call themselves *Zacha* from the Name of one of their ancient Princes. But the Name of that Prince who headed them, at the Time when they separated from *Bratti*, who live near the *Baikallian Lake* which were formerly united as one Nation, was *Deptzi Tarchan tegin*. They do not worship *Bulhwani*, or Idols carved in Wood, like the *Ostiaks* and *Tungusi*; But they offer Sacrifices to an invisible GOD in Heaven; Yet they have a Type or Image of that Deity stuffed out, with a monstrous Head, Eyes of Corral, and a Body like a Bag; this Image they hang upon a Tree, and round it the Furs of Sables and other Animals. Each Tribe has one of these Images. Their Priests, whom they call *Bihun*, make use of Drums, like the *Laplanders*; they worship the INVISIBLE GOD, under three different Denominations, *Artoyon*, *Schugstoygon*, and *Tangara*, which three Names, are called by them *Sunnans* (i. e. *Sacred*.) What *Isbrand Ides* (in his Travels, p. 132.) relates, concerning these People, is all true; excepting the Custom of burying alive, or killing the oldest Servants, or Favourites of a Prince, at his Funeral, which is abolish'd; But they still own, that formerly, before the *Russians* were amongst them, they were used to do so. They have besides, many superstitious Customs, in common with other Nations, which they celebrate about certain Trees, that they look upon to be sacred: When they meet with a fine Tree, they presently hang all Manner of Nick-Nacks about it, as Iron,

‡ The natural and civil History of *Kamtschatka*, translated from the Original, published in the *Russian* Language at *Petersburg*, being just ready for the Press, we shall defer giving any Account of that Country here.

(iii)

It was therefore already decided, that there was no Connection between the two Parts of the World; but this had been forgotten. Such a remarkable

Iron, Brass, Copper, &c. Their Priests, or *Bihunt*, when they perform their superstitious Rites, put on a Garment trim'd with Bits of Iron, Rattles and Bells. As soon as the Fields begin to be green, each Generation gathers together, at a Place where there is a fine Tree, and a pleasant Spot of Ground. There they sacrifice Horses and Oxen (as a New Year's Offering, their New Year beginning in *April*,) the Heads of which they stick up round the Trees, and on the Heads of the former they leave the Skin. They then take a certain Liquor, which they call *Cumifs*, sit down in a Circle, and after having lifted up the Jugg, with both Hands, they drink to one another: Then they dip a Brush in the *Cumises* and sprinkle some in the Air, and some into the Fire, which they light up, on that Occasion. On this Festival they get wretchedly drunk, and gorge themselves to that degree with Meat, that it is said four Persons will commonly devour a whole Horse. Nay some will strip themselves stark naked, that nothing may confine or hinder them from extending their Paunches; This they continue so long, till some breathe their last on the Spot. These People are very nasty; They seldom or hardly ever, wash themselves; they will eat the Flesh of Oxen, Cows, and Horses, but no Pork, be they never so hungry: But then they never mind whether the Cattle be sick or sound; for they indifferently kill and eat it. If the Meat has had but one boiling up, it is done enough for them; they never skim the Pot, but look upon the Skum to be the fattest and best Part of all, and therefore distribute it about, as a great Dainty. The Vessels in which they stamp their dried Fish, Roots, and Berries, are made of dried Oxen and Cow's Dung. Their Cattle stand in the same Room, or Hut, where they themselves dwell; the Floor of their Huts is terrassed even and smooth. They eat Bread, when they can get it, but it is no usual Part of their Diet, because they neither Plough, Sow, nor Plant. They eat but little Salt, yet sometimes they take Salt in Exchange for other Commodities. They are fond of smoaking *Chinese Schaar*, or Tobacco, for which they truck with the *Russians*. In *February* and *March* is their Harvest, when the Sap rises in the Trees; for then they go into the Woods, cut down young Pine-Trees, take off the inner Bark or Bast, which they carry home and dry for their Winter's Provision. They then beat it to a fine Powder, boil it in Milk, and eat it together with dried Fish, also beat to Powder. They shift their Habitations, in the same Manner, as the *Tobolskian Tartars* do. Their Winter-Houses or Huts, are square, made of thin Planks and Beams; The Roof is covered with Earth, and a Hole is left, in the Middle, for the Smoke to go out. Their Summer-Dwellings are round, and in Shape of a Sugar-Loaf; the Out-side Shell of these Huts is made of the Bark of Birch-Trees, curiously joined together, and embroider'd with Horse-Hair died of many Colours. A Hole is also left at the Top, for the Smoak to pass through. They make their Chimnies or Fire-Places, in the Middle of their Huts, where they also fix a Pot-Hook to hang their Pots on, which they make themselves, as they also do their Kettles, which have only an Iron Bottom, the Sides being made of the Bark of Birch, which they have a Way of joining to that Iron Bottom so tight and close, that it will not only hold Water, but that the Flame of the Fire cannot burn it. They bury their Dead divers Ways: The most Eminent among them pitch upon a fine Tree, and declare that they will be buried there; and when the Corpse is buried, they put some of the best Moveables of the deceased, along with him, into his Grave. Some only put the Corpse upon a Board, which they fix upon four Posts, in the Wood, cover the dead Body with an Ox's or Horse's Hide, and so leave it. Some again put the Body into the Ground. But the greater Part of them, when they die, are left in their Huts, whence the Relations take the most valuable Things, make the Huts up close, and then leave them. Those who die in the City of *Jakuhtskoi*, are left lying in the Streets, where they are frequently devoured by Dogs. Each Tribe of these People looks upon some particular Creature as Sacred, *e. g.* a
Swan,

markable Event would perhaps have been for ever concealed, if I had not, in the Year 1736, had the Happiness, during my Stay at *Jakutzk*, to find in the Archives of the Town Originals in Writing, in which this Voyage is described, with Circumstances that leave no Room for Doubt.

In the Year 1636, they began to navigate the Frozen Sea from *Jakutzk*. The Rivers *Jana*, *Indigirka*, *Alasca*, *Kolyma*, came to be known one after the other. The first Navigation from the River *Kolyma* towards the East, was made in the Year 1646, by a Company of Volunteers, who were called *Promyschleni*. They found the Sea full of Ice, yet between the Ice and the Continent a free navigable Water, in which they sailed for twice twenty-four Hours together. A Bay between the Rocks on the Coast gave an Opportunity of entering it. They found People of the Nation of the *Tschuktschi*. With these they dealt in this Manner. The Merchandize was exposed upon the Strand; the *Tschukschi* took

Swan, Goose, Raven, &c. and such is not eaten by that Tribe, though the others may eat it. As to their Tongue there is some Affinity between them and the *Crim Tartars*: and a Conformity with the Tongues of the *Bratti*, the *Kirgasi*, and the *Sajantzian Tartars*; though the last talk pretty commonly the *Mungalian* and *Kalmuchkian* Tongues, to which Countries they are near Neighbours. The *Jakuhti*, like other Pagans, allow of Polygamy. They buy and sell their Wives, as it is customary among the *Tartars* and *Ostiacki*, and all their Neighbours: Where the Bridegroom is obliged to purchase his Bride of her Parents.

Jakutzk, is Capital of this Province, on the River *Lena*, distant above a hundred *German* Miles from the Frozen Sea. There resides a Governor-General. The Soil about this City, notwithstanding it lies pretty far North, produces Corn. However, the Inhabitants, who are more intent upon hunting Sables, Foxes, and other Animals, for the Sake of their Furs, neglect cultivating what they call *Stari paschni Teldun*, (i. e. the Land which their Forefathers used to plough.) Another Reason why they are remiss in this Point is, their having an Opportunity of being supplied with Corn, by Means of the Rivers *Wittim* and *Kiringa*, the Banks of which produce fine Corn: But though very little Corn is sown in this Country, yet that which is, whatever Grain it be of, thrives apace; but the Straw never exceeds six Inches in Height; for as soon as the Corn peeps out of the Ground, it immediately shoots into Ears, and ripens in six Weeks Time. The Reason of this is, because here the Sun is hardly ever below the Horizon in Summer, but affords its cherishing Warmth, both Night and Day, to the Ground: And what is most observable, is, that during that whole Time, it does not rain; but the Earth, though fat and black, yet never thaws above six or nine Inches deep; insomuch that the Roots are plentifully supplied with Moisture from below, whilst the constant Heat of the Sun above, irradiates what is out of the Ground; and this is the Cause of so quick a Harvest: On the other hand, those Places which are situated more Westward, do not enjoy this Advantage: The high Icy Mountains of the Island of *Nova Zembla* lying just opposite to them. Near this City are bred also very good Horses; they are pretty large, are used to be turned out all the Winter long, and will scrape the Snow with their Hoofs aside, to come at the Grass; they also eat the Studs of Birch and Aspen, and grow sleik, plump, and fat, and look much better than they do in Summer, when their Hair grows long. Not far from this City, Westward, there runs a River called *Wilgui*, near the Head of which there is a Vulcano. The Ashes thrown up by this Mountain are looked upon to be the *Flores Salis Armoniaci*.

(v)

took what pleased them, and put in lieu of them Sea-horse Teeth, or Things made of them. Nobody would venture to go ashore to the *Tschuktschi*; and besides an Interpreter was wanted, as they did not understand each other's Language. They were content with having made this first Discovery, and returned to the River *Kolyma*.

Upon their Return, the Intelligence relating to the Teeth of the Seahorse, inticed more of the *Promyschleni* to undertake a second Voyage the following Year. These were joined by *Fedot Alexeew*; but he found it requisite to desire the Governor upon the River *Kolyma*, to allow him to have a *Cossac* that was in his Service to take Care of the Interest of the Crown during the Voyage. For this Purpose, one *Semun Deschnew* offered himself, and was furnished with Orders from he Governor. Four Ships that were called Kotsches sailed at once, in *June* 1647, from the River *Kolyma*. People had heard of the River *Anadir*, which was reported to be well inhabited; and it was believed, that it emptied itself into the Frozen Ocean; consequently, one of the Views of this Voyage was to discover its Mouth: But not only this, but every Thing else that was proposed to be done, miscarried; because the Sea was that Summer too full of Ice to permit of a free Navigation.

The Hopes conceived were, however, not abandoned; on the contrary, the Number of the Favourers of this Project, as well among the *Cossacs* as *Promyschleni*, encreased the following Year in such a Manner, that seven Kotsches were equipped all with the same View. What became of four of these Vessels is unknown: on board the remaining three were *Semun Deschnew* and *Gerasim Ankudinow*, the Chiefs of the *Cossacs*, and *Fedot Alexeew*, the Chief among the *Promyschleni*. The 20th of *June*, 1648, was the Day on which this remarkable Voyage began. It is to be regretted, as we have but yet little Knowledge of those Parts, that all the Circumstances of this Navigation are not mentioned. *Deschnew*, who, in an Account sent to *Jakutzk*, relates his Adventures, seems to speak only accidentally of what happened to him by Sea. To the great Isthmus of *Tschuktschi*, we find no Events mentioned. No Notice is taken of Obstructions by the Ice; and probably there were none; for *Deschnew* observes, upon another Occasion, that the Sea is not usually so clear of Ice as it was at this Time. His Relation begins with the great Isthmus, which indeed is a Circumstance that deserves the most Notice. "This Isthmus, says he, is quite different from
" that which is found by the River *Tschukotschia*, West of the
" River *Kolyma*. It lies between the North, and North East,
" and turns circular towards the River *Anadir*. On the *Russian*,
" that

"that is, the West Side of it, there falls a Brook into the Sea, by
"which the *Tschuktschi* have erected a Scaffold like a Tower of
"the Bones of Whales. Overagainst the Isthmus (it is not men-
"tioned on which Side) there are two Islands in the Sea, upon which
"were seen People of the *Tschuktschi* Nation, thro' whose Lips were
"run Pieces of the Teeth of the Sea-horse. One might sail from the
"Isthmus to the River *Anadir*, with a fair Wind, in three Days and
"Nights, and it might be travelled by Land within the same Time,
"since the River *Anadir* empties itself into a Bay." Mean while,
at this Isthmus it was, that *Ankudinow's* Kotsche was wrecked, and her
Crew saved on board the other Kotsches. *Deschnew* and *Fedot Alexeew*
were ashore on the 20th of *September*, and had an Engagement with
the *Tschuktschi*, in which the latter was wounded. The two Kotsches
lost Sight of one another, and did not rejoin each other again. *Deschnew* was driven about in the Sea by the Wind and Waves till *October*.
At last he suffered Shipwreck, as appears by Circumstances, pretty far
to the South of the River *Anadir*, about the River *Olutora*. What
became of *Fedot Alexeew* and his Ship's Company will be afterwards
mentioned.

Deschnew had twenty-five Men, with whom he went in Search of
the *Anadir*; but for Want of a Guide, he did not find it till after he
had travelled ten Weeks on Foot. The Place where he reached that
River was not far from its Mouth, and had no Inhabitants or Woods.
Twelve Men of the Company went up the *Anadir*; but, after twenty
Days, they were obliged to return to the Place where *Deschnew* had
fixed his Habitation, which, from the Effects of Hunger and Fatigue,
few of them were able to reach.

The following Summer, 1649, *Deschnew* with his Company went
up the *Anadir* by Water, and found a People who called themselves
Anauli. He obliged them, after destroying great Numbers, to pay
the Tribute; and founded *Anadirskoi Ostrog*, where he fixed his Residence.

People were not idle after *Deschnew's* Departure for the River *Kolyma*, in regulating new Expeditions, as well by Water as by Land. A-
mongst these, one made by Sea deserves to be taken Notice of; not so
much on Account of the Discoveries made thereby, as from what occasioned it.

Michael Staduchin, Cossac of *Jakutzk*, with some of his Companions,
had built in the Year 1644, the lowermost *Ostrog* on the River *Kolyma*,
and the Year following returned to *Jakutzk*, with some Accounts which
seem to deserve Examination. He was told that there is a great Island

in

in the Frozen Sea, which extends from the River *Jana* opposite to *Kolyma*; and could be observed from the Continent. The *Tschuktschi* of the River *Tschukotschia*, which falls into the Frozen Sea to the Westward of *Kolyma*, used to go with Rein Deer in the Winter in one Day's time to this Island, there to kill Sea-horses, the Heads and Teeth of which they brought back, and worshiped them. Indeed *Staduchin* himself had not seen such Teeth among the People; but he had heard from the *Promyschleni* that such were found among them, and that certain Rings belonging to the Sledges of their Rein Deer were made of the Teeth of Sea-horses. The *Promyschleni* also confirmed the Reality of such an Island, and held it for a Continuation of the Land of *Nova Zembla*, whither they used to go from *Mesen*.

Upon these Advices, *Staduchin* was on the 5th of *June*, 1647, dispatch'd for the second Time. He could neither discover nor procure any farther Intelligence of the Island in the Frozen Sea, and after some fruitless Researches, the most important Fruit he reap'd from this Voyage was the Information he brought, that the nearest Way to the *Anadir* was by Land. This gave Occasion to the following Expedition. Properly the advantageous Intelligence of a Way by Land to the River *Anadir*, was owing to a Campaign made by the *Cossacs* from the *Kolyma* up the river *Anui*, in the Beginning of the Year, 1650. What was known before, consisted only in an uncertain Report; but here Prisoners were taken from the *Chodynzi*, who were well acquainted with the Way.

Immediately a Company of Volunteers joined, composed partly of *Cossacs*, and partly of *Promyschleni*, who desired the Commander *Kolymskoi Ostrog*, to let them go to the River *Anadir*, to render the People there tributary. This was done. *Semoen Motora* the Leader of this Company, took Prisoner on the 23d of *March*, on the upper Part of the River *Anui*, a Person of Distinction belonging to the *Chodynzi*, whom he carried along with him to the *Anadir*. *Motora* on the 23d of *April*, 1650, arrived at the *Anadir*, where he was joined by *Deschnew*; and followed by *Michailo Staduchin*, who, jealous of the others, left them, and went to the *Penschina*, after which nothing farther was ever heard of him.

Deschnew and *Motora* had built Vessels on the *Anadir*, to put to Sea with them, in order to discover more Rivers, when the Death of the latter happened; for in the End of the Year 1651, he lost his Life in an Engagement with the *Anaules*. In the mean while *Deschnew* sail'd in the Summer 1652, to the Mouth of the River *Anadir*, where he observed, that on the North Side of it, a Sand-bank extended itself far into

into the Sea: On the Mouth of this River, plenty of Sea-horses are found: *Deschnew* got several of their Teeth, and thereby thought himself sufficiently rewarded for his Labour.

In the Year 1653, he had Wood felled to build a Kotsche, in which he might send the Tribute he had received to *Jakutzk*: But as other Materials were wanting, this Affair did not go on. It was likewise said, that the Sea about the great *Tschuktschi Nofs*, was not every Year free from Ice.

A second Voyage to the *Korga*, on Account of the Sea-horse Teeth, was made in the Year 1654, at which was also present *Juchko Seliwerstow*, a *Coffac*, lately come from *Jakutzk*, who had accompanied *Michail Staduchin* in his Voyage, and being sent by him to *Jakutzk*, with a Proposal to have a Search made after the Sea-horse Teeth, was now provided with an Order for that Purpose. In his Instructions, next to *Anadir*, is also named the River *Jentschendon*, which empties itself into the Bay of *Penshinsky*. On these two he was to make the People tributary, because the Transactions of *Deschnew* at *Jakutzk* were not yet known. This occasioned new Discontents: *Seliwerstow* wanted to ascribe to himself the Discovery of the *Korga*, as if this was the Place where he had arrived by Sea with *Staduchin* in the Year 1649; but *Deschnew* proved that they had not so much as reached the great Nofs of *Tchutktchy*, which consisted of nothing but Rocks, and was but too well known to him, since *Ankudinow*'s Kotche was wrecked there. "This, said he, was not the first Cape which occurred under the "Name of *Swatoi* Nofs. The Islands where the Teeth are found, "situated opposite the Nofs of *Tchuktchy*, were the proper Mark "thereof. These Men *Deschnew* had seen; but *Maduchin* and *Seli-* "*werstow* had not; and the *Korga* on the Mouth of the River *Anadir*, "was not far from it."

Deschnew taking at the same Time a View of the Sea Coast, found *Korjakish* ‖ Habitations, and in them a *Jakutzk* Woman, whom he knew

to

‖ *Korjaki*, or *Karaiki*, are a Pagan Nation, living on the West and North Side of the Country of *Kamtschatka*. They are beardless, like the *Luplanders*, *Samojeds*, and *Ostiaks*; for, in the first Place, they have naturally very little Hair about the Mouth, and what little they have they pluck out, as do also the *Jakuhti*, *Tungusi* and *Kalmucks*. They are naturally a good harmless People, and have no Idols of Stone, Wood, or any other Materials, as the *Ostiaks* have. They use no Manner of Ceremony in their Devotion; but when they go out a Hunting, they pray to the SUPREME BEING to bless them with Success. However, they have their *Schamans* or Magicians, and are a very filthy People. They do not build their Huts on the Ground, but upon four Posts, like some *Armenians*, and get up, by means of a Ladder, to the Top, where they enter through a Hole. For their necessary Occasions they make use of a Tub, which they have with them in the Hut, and, when full, they carry

(ix)

to have belonged to *Fedot Alexeew*. He asked her where her Master was? She answered, "*Fedot* and *Gerasim (Ankudinow)* died of the "Scurvy; others of their Company were slain, and a few had saved "themselves by Flight, in small Vessels, without any Body's knowing "what was become of them." Of these latter Vestiges were afterwards discovered on the River *Kamtschatka*.

When *Wolodimer Atlassow*, in the Year 1697, laid the Foundation of the Conquest of the Country of *Kamtschatka*, the *Russians* were already known to its Inhabitants. It is a common Report among the *Kamtschedales*, that long before *Atlassow*, a certain Fedotow, who, probably, was the Son of *Fedot Alexeew*, had, with some of his Comrades lived amongst them, and intermarried with their *Kamtschedale* Women: they still shewed the Place of the *Russian* Habitations, and the Mouth of the small River *Nikul*, which falls into the *Kamtschatka*, and therefore in the *Russian* Language is called *Fedoticha*. But at *Atlassow*'s Arrival, none of these first *Russians* were left. They are said to have been so much honoured that they were almost deify'd. It was not believed that a human Hand could hurt them, but after the *Russians* began to quarrel among themselves, and one wounding the other, so that the *Kamtschedales* saw the Blood flow from them; after their separating from each other, and some of them going over to the Sea of *Penschinsky*, they were all slain, partly by the *Kamtschedales*, partly by the *Korjakes*. The River *Fedotcha* falls into the River *Kamtschatka* on the South Side, 180 Werfts * below *Werchni Kamtchatzkoi Ostrog*. Upon this River *Fedoticha* were seen, at the Time of the first Expedition of *Kamtschatka*, the Ruins

carry it out, and make use of the same Tub to bring in Water, for other Occasions: A whole Family will lie all naked together under one large Coverlet. The *Russians* who trade with them, carry thither a Kind of Mushrooms, called, in the *Russian* Tongue, *Muchomor*, which they exchange for Squirils, Fox, Ermin, Sable, and other Furs: Those who are rich among them, lay up large Provisions of these Mushrooms, for the Winter. When they make a Feast, they pour Water upon some of these Mushrooms, and boil them. They then drink the Liquor, which intoxicates them; the poorer Sort, who cannot afford to lay in a Store of these Mushrooms, post themselves, on these Occasions, round the Huts of the Rich, and watch the Opportunity of the Guests coming down to make Water, and then hold a Wooden Bowl to receive the Urin, which they drink off greedily, as having still some Virtue of the Mushroom in it, and by this Way they also get drunk. In Spring and Summer they catch a large Quantity of Fish, and digging Holes in the Ground, which they line with the Bark of Birch, they fill them with it, and cover the Holes over with Earth. As soon as they think the Fish is rotten and tender, they take out some of it, pour Water upon it, and boil it with red-hot Pebbles (as the *Finlandians* do their Beer) and feed upon it, as the greatest Delicacy in the World. This Mess stinks so abominably, that the *Russians* who deal with them, and who are none of the most squeamish, are themselves not able to endure it. Of this Liquor they likewise drink so immoderately, that they will be quite intoxicated, or drunk with it.

* Versta, or Werst, is a *Russian* Measure of Land, used instead of Miles, of 500 Satches, or *Russian* Fathoms; 104 1-5th Wersts are equal to a Degree of 69½ *English* Miles.

b
of

of two Simowies, wherein *Fedotow* with his Companions, is said to have lived; but nobody could tell the Way by which these first *Ruffians* came to *Kamtschatka*. This was not known till the Year 1736, when the Particulars of this Affair were found in the Archives of *Jakutzk*.

Concerning the pretended great Island in the *Frozen Sea*, of which Mention has been made on Occasion of the Voyage of *Michailo Staduchin*, the *Coffack*, that in the Year 1645 an Account had been received of it, which was not then confirmed. It is first to be observed, that in all Descriptions of Voyages between the Rivers *Lena* and *Kolyma*, of which there are a considerable Number in the Archives of *Jakutzk*, not one mentions a Word of this great Island, although several Vessels have been driven by contrary Winds so far into the Sea, that they must necessarily have seen it, if there had been any such Island. To prove this, two Voyages may serve, made in 1650, partly by one and the same Company; so that the Accounts of the one may serve as a Confirmation of those of the other. One may likewise gather from them, with what Toil and Danger these Voyages were accompanied.

Andrei Goreloi, a *Coffac*, was dispatched from *Jakutzk* in July 1650, to go by Sea to the River *Indigirka* and to render tributary the People dwelling above this, and the River *Moma*, which falls into the *Indigirka*. He sailed so far successfully, that on the last Day of *August* he came over against the Mouth of the River *Chroma*. There he was frozen in, according to his Account, two Days Voyage from the Continent, when he should have gone to it on Foot over the Ice: but he was not so happy: the Ice broke up again, and a violent Tempest which lasted ten Days, drove his Kotsche still farther into the Sea, where he was froze in again, and had a Journey of a Fortnight over the Ice on Foot, to the Land. In the mean while the Kotsche was wreck'd between the Ice. *Goreloi* and his Men had drawn with him upon Sledges, some of the Naval Stores and Provisions; but left great Part in the Sea. From the Place where they reached the Continent, they set out with Sledges drawn by Dogs *, on the 5th of *October*, and came in four Days to the Mouth

---

* Dogs, are very scarce in *China*, nor will they thrive there: wherefore Merchants and Travellers who go from *Ruffia* thither, commonly carry some with them, which turn to a very good Account, especially if they are broke, and have learned some Tricks. On the other Hand, there are at *Thibet* and *Tanguht*, Dogs of a vast Size: This seems to agree with what *Marcus Paulus* relates of the large Dogs in *Tanguhtia*, as also with that Passage in *Arianus*, and *Quintus Curtius*, where they mention, that King *Porus* made a present of two of these large Dogs to *Alexander*. On the East Side of the Country of *Kamtschatki*, towards the Sea, there lives a People, who keep no other Sorts of Beasts but Dogs, which though they

Mouth of the River *Indigirka*, and from thence, on the 12th of *November* to *Ujandina Simowei*, where a Poud§ of Meal cost eight Rubles¶, on account of the many Misfortunes that happened by Sea, and no Corn being sent thither.

The second Voyage to be brought here as a Proof, was that of *Timofei Buldakow*, a Cossac; who, in 1649, was sent as Commander to the River *Kolyma*, but had passed the Winter at *SeLigani*, on the River *Lena*. He came the 2d of *July*, 1650, to the Mouth of the River, and sailed to the Gulph of *Omoloewa*. There he met with Ice, and was driven between it for eight Days together in the Sea. Near one of the Islands, formed by the several Branches of the *Lena*, he was obliged to beat his Way through the Ice, for two Days, in order to reach it. At last it seemed as if the Sea was quite free from Ice; wherefore *Buldakow* sailed again towards the Gulph of *Omoloewa*; but there found still great Shoals of Ice, among which he drove about in the Sea four

b 2 Days

they are but of a common Size, are remarkable, in that they have Hair of six Inches long. In 1718, a certain *Waiwode* travelling in a sledge with twelve dogs, towards the City of *Berefown*, got himself wrapped up in warm Quilts, and girt fast in the Sledge, in order to secure him from the Severity of the Cold, and to prevent his falling out, in case the Sledge should over-turn; the *Ostiack*, who was his Guide, skaited along Side of him, (according to Custom, in case the Sledge should over-turn, to raise it up again) and coming on a large Plain, where the Ground is generally covered Man's Depth with Snow, the Dogs (which the *Ostiacks* also use for Hunting) espying a Fox at a Distance, immediately flew in Pursuit of their Game, and run away with the *Waiwode*, with such Swiftness, that it was impossible for the Guide to keep pace with them, and they soon got out of Sight. The Guide followed the Track, but did not come up to his Passenger till the next Morning, when he found him in the Sledge overturned, still well wrapped up, and tightly girt into it. By good Luck, a stump of a Tree, which stood out above the Snow, had stopped the Sledge, or else it might probably have cost the *Waiwode* his Life. These Dogs are able to draw great Burthens, for, in the Year 1718, Governor *Knees Mischewski* ordered a whole Pipe of Brandy to be brought from the Convent of *Kesfkoe* to the City of *Berefow*, which was done by sixteen Dogs. People never travel a Nights, but only a Days with Dogs: In the Morning, before they set out, each Dog has two frozen Fish, which is his Allowance for the whole Day. At Night, when they come to their Journey's End, these poor Creatures are so weary, that they cannot eat, but presently lie down to sleep. Whenever any Passenger comes to a Stage, where he is to have fresh Dogs, all the Dogs of that Village set up a most terrible Howling, knowing that they are, some of them, to have the same Fate.

§ Poud, a *Russian* Weight, of forty *Russian*, or about thirty-six *English* Pounds.

¶ Rubel, is a *Russian* Silver Coin, about the Size of a Crown Piece, in Value ten Guilders, or one hundred Kopeiks; two Rubels are of equal Value with a Ducat. They go generally in *Holland* for fifty-five or sixty Stivers, according as the Exchange runs. Formerly they had no other Coin in *Russia* but Denga's (of the Value of half a Kopeik,) and their way of Reckoning was to have a Tally, and at the Sum of every hundred Denga's, they cut a Notch upon the Tally, which Notch they called Rubel, and, therefore, when they afterward coined Silver Coin, of just one hundred Kopeiks in Value, they called it a Rubel, or Notch.

Days more. There were no Hopes of his getting forward; his sole Endeavour was therefore to get rid of the Ice, in order to return to the *Lena*. At the Mouth of the *Lena* there lay eight Kotsches manned partly with *Cossacs*, partly with Merchants and *Promyschleni*, and ready to put to Sea. Soon after a Land-wind arose which removed the Ice; when all the nine Kotsches passed the Gulph of *Omoloewa* at the same Time. Beyond this Gulph lies an Island near the Land, behind which was, at that Time, the usual Navigation. When they were going to enter the Streights that separated the Island from the Continent, they found a Shoal of Ice fixed to the Bottom of the Sea, and could no otherwise pass through it than by all the Crews of the several Vessels joining to remove this Obstruction. In the Streights behind the Island the Kotsches were drawn by Men; and after Twenty-four Hours Navigation in the Streights, a favourable Wind began to blow, which brought them in Twenty-four Hours more to the Mouth of the river *Yana*. Here a Wind from the Sea brought such a quantity of Ice together, that it almost squeezed the Kotches to pieces. But as the Coasts of the Frozen Sea are in these Parts sloping, so that the great Shoals of Ice which sink deep in the Water, cannot come nigh the Shore, they work'd themselves happily through near the Land, and on the 29th of *August* passed the Cape, which formerly, on Account of its northerly Situation was reckoned to be the most difficult Place in this Voyage, and therefore was called *Swatoi Noss*. They were nearly opposite the Mouth of the River *Chroma*; when in the Night between the 30th and 31st of *August*, the Sea was frozen quite over. *Bulldakow*'s and four other Kotsches that were not far from the Shore, having but one Fathom Water, thought as soon as the Ice would be strong enough to transport their Effects over it to the Land; but these Hopes vanished; since on the First of *September*, when the Ice was already half a Span thick, a violent Wind from the Land arose, and bore the Ice up again, driving the Kotsches between the Ice into the open Sea, which took up five Days. There afterwards being a Calm, the Sea froze again in one Night, and on the third Day the Ice was so thick, that they might pass over it. People were then sent out to take a Survey on which Side was the nearest Land; when it was found that Kotche commanded by *Andrei Gorcloi*, was a Day's Voyage more to the South than the other Kotsches, of which there were five, including his. Wherefore, for the present, they embarked with their Provisions and other Necessaries, on board *Gorcloi*'s Kotsche, that in case the Sea should break up again, the way to the Continent might be so much the shorter; but when every thing was ready for beginning the Voyage, the Sea suddenly

(xiii)

denly begun to fwell; the Ice, which was already half an Arfchin * thick, broke in Pieces, and a ftrong Wind drove the Kotfches ftill farther into the Sea than before. This again lafted five Days; after which the Wind ceafed, and the Kotfches froze in a third Time. They were obliged to leave them, and proceed on foot over the Ice to the Continent, every one taking upon a fmall Sledge, as much Provifions and Implements with him as he could draw. But even now they had much Danger and Fatigue to undergo; the Ice often broke under their Feet; they were often obliged to leap from one Shoal of Ice to another; to throw over their Provifions and Implements, and to pull one another over with great Poles and Ropes. At laft they arrived at the Shore, near the Mouth of the *Indigirka*, and proceeded up the River to *Ujando, Simowie*, &c.

Two Years after, viz. in 1652, we find the Inftructions of one *Piatidefatniks Iwan Rebrow*, who, in *Buldakow*'s Room, was fent as Commander to the River *Kolyma*, to inform himfelf of the abovementioned great Ifland in the Frozen Sea, of which all was repeated to him that *Michailo Staduchin* had reported. And it is poffible that the fame Thing was afterwards enjoined to the *Kolymifh* and other Commanders there. But this is certain, that in the Archives of *Jakutzk* no Accounts of Difcoveries that have followed thereupon are to be met with; and fo the Affair might reft here, if of late it had not been brought upon the Carpet again, and by exprefs Expeditions had been treated in fuch a Manner, that the Reality of the faid Ifland feems to have gained fome Appearance of Credit.

On *February* 20, 1710, the following Account was taken down in Writing, in the Chancery of *Jakutzk*, upon the Interrogation and Depofition of feveral Coffacs of *Jakutzk*, in relation to that and other Iflands fituated oppofite to the Land of *Kamtfchatka*.

Nikiphar Mulgin faid, that in the Time of the *Waywode* of *Jakutzk*, *Knjas Iwan Petrowitfch Borjatinfkoi*, (who, from 1667 to 1675, had prefided in the Government of *Jakutzk*) had failed by Sea with a Merchant named *Andrei Woripaew*, from the *Lena* to the River *Kolyma*; during which Voyage they had moftly failed along the Continent as far as *Swjatoi Nofs*; but afterwards, on Account of the great Quantity of Ice faftened to the Shore, they had been obliged to keep out from Sea. In this Voyage, the Pilot of their Kotfche had fhewn the whole Company, at a great Diftance, an Ifland on this Side of the Mouth of
the

---

* Arfchin, i. a *Ruffian* Meafure, twenty-eight Inches long, and is divided into fixteen Werfchock, or Parts, fo that each Quarter of this Meafure contains four Werfchocks; three Arfchin make a Sazohen or *Ruffian* Fathom.

the River *Kolyma*, which every body was able to discern: And after their coming to the *Kolyma*, a Merchant, named *Jacob Wjatka*, had told them in what Manner nine Kotfches in Company, had failed from the *Lena* to the *Kolyma*, when three of these Vessels were driven to that Island. The People that were sent ashore, observed the Impression of the Hoofs of unknown Beasts, but saw no Inhabitants: These Kotfches arrived at *Kolyma*; but of an Island situated opposite the Mouth of the River *Lena*, he had never heard, &c.

This Deposition contains also an Account of an Island, supposed to lie opposite the Country of *Kamtschatka*, but with so many uncertain Circumstances, that it requires a good Explanation, if the Accounts published afterwards are to be rendered consistent with it. *Taras Staduchin*, a Merchant, is said to have told *Malgin*, that many Years ago he sailed with ninety Men in a Kotfche from the River *Kolyma*, to make Discoveries in relation to the great Cape of *Tschuktschy*; that they could not double it, but went over it on Foot; and on the other Side, where they built new Vessels, in which, sailing along the Coasts, they came to the Mouth of the River *Penschina*. There the Narrowness of the Place they crossed over is most remarkable: But going farther, said, that opposite the Mouth of the *Penschina*, we may see in the Sea an Island, and that the same Island, according to the Relation of a Woman, whom they took Prisoner, is inhabited by People who have great Beards, wear long Cloaths, and call the *Russians*, Brethren. These are the Circumstances that want a good Explanation.

First, It is possible that the Name of the River *Penschina* may have been put by mistake instead of the River *Kamtschatka*; for, as improbable as it is that *Staduchin* should have sailed all round *Kamtschatka* to the River *Penschina* in one Voyage, so certain is it on the other Hand, that opposite to *Penschina*, there is no Island to be met with in the Sea: And altho' there is none to be seen from the Mouth of the River *Kamtschatka*, yet the *Kamtschedales* may have had an Account of the Islands that are known in those Parts. The great Beards and long Cloaths that are to shew a Similitude with the *Russians*, seem to be borrowed from the Nation of the *Kurilles*, who inhabit the Islands situated to the South of *Kamtschatka*: as indeed these, contrary to the Nature of all the People of *Siberia* and *Kamtschatka*, are bearded, and hairy on their bodies: But it is a Mistake that they call the *Russians* Brethren: At the Time of *Taras Staduchin*, the *Kurilles* had perhaps never heard of the *Russians*. *Staduchin*, it may be concluded, the Brotherhood, from the similar Form of Body; and *Malgin*, from a Mistake of Memory, may have ascribed it to the *Kamtschedales*.

Iwan

Iwan Schamaew, said, That in the Year 1700, he was sent to *Kamtschatka*, with *Timofei Kobelew*, the Commander of that Country: they making use of Rein Deer, from *Anadirsk* to the River *Penschina*, where they built Vessels and sailed with them by Sea to *Pustoi Ostrog*, probably on the River *Pustaia*, where again they got Rein Deer, with which they passed over a Chain of Mountains to the River *Kamtschatka*; opposite the Mouth of the River *Penschina*, there was a little Island in the Sea. At last, in the Return from *Kamtschatka*, he had seen an Island opposite the Mouth of the River *Karaga*, on which the *Cossac Iwan Golygin* had been with two others, at the Distance of a Day's rowing from the Continent to the Island, where they found Inhabitants; but these refusing to pay Tribute, they did not venture to go far upon the Island, or to take a minute Account of it.

Michailo Nasetkin said, that in the Year 1702, he had been sent to *Kamtschatka*; Their Way had been, as in the former Journey, by *Anadirsk* to the River *Penschina*, from whence they went by Water to the River *Lesnaia*, and from thence by Land with Sledges to the River *Kamtschatka*. At the Mouth of this River might be seen at a Distance in the Sea, an Island; but it was uncertain whether it was inhabited or not, and that the *Russians* had never been upon it. From the South Promontory of *Kamtschatka*, he had seen Islands or Land, such as he had likewise observed on his return to *Jakutzk*, when he sailed by Sea, between the Rivers *Kolyma* and *Indigirka*. This last Land, or Island, is, according to the Account of the Pilot *Danilo Monastirskoi*, who at that Time was with them, is contiguous to the Land, situated opposite to *Kamtschatka*, and extends opposite to the Mouth of the River *Lena*; but whether the Land was inhabited or not, that Pilot was entirely ignorant.

Alexei Porotow, who in the Year 1704, had been at *Kamtschatka*, has said the same of the Island overagainst the Mouth of the River *Karaga*, as *Iwan Schamaew*.

Here ends the Interrogations in the Chancery of *Jakutzk*.

At the same Time the *Stolnick* and Chief Commandant *Knjas Wasilei Iwanowitch Gagarin*, was present at *Jakutzk*, being dispatched to *Siberia* from the Governor *Knjas Matfei Petrowitsch Gagarin*, his Father's Brother, with full Power to make Discoveries and better Regulations. On the 17th of *March* he delivered an Order to the *Waywode Trauernicht*, consisting of several Points, one of which was as follows: " That he " should make diligent Enquiry about the Islands situated opposite the " Mouth of the River *Kolyma*, and the Land of *Kamtschatka*, what " People inhabited them; under whose Jurisdiction they were; what

was

"was their Employment; how large the Islands were, and how far
"distant from the Continent." With which Enquiries the Commanders and *Cossacs* who were to be sent to those Places were commissioned, with Promise that they might expect a particular Reward for this Service from his *Czarish* Majesty, to whom an Account should be sent of what had been done, by an Express.

In consequence of this, Orders were at first given, dated the 20th of *Aug.* and 9th of *Sept.* 1710, to the Commanders of *Ust-Jana* and *Kolyma*, from the Chancery of *Jakutzk*, to make these Discoveries their particular Business; upon which a Deposition in Writing was received from *Jacob Permakow*, a *Cossac* of *Ust-Jana*, which mentioned that he once sailed from the *Lena*, to the River *Kolyma*; and that on the farther Side of the *Swatoi Ness*, he had seen an Island in the Sea; but did not know whether it was inhabited or not. There was likewise situated directly opposite the River *Kolyma*, an Island that might be seen from the Continent, and Mountains were observed upon it; but that it was also uncertain whether it had any Inhabitance: this perhaps might be known from the *Jukagiri*, who dwelt thereabouts.*

A Letter from the Governor *Knjas Matfei Petrowitsch Gagarin*, of the 28th of *Jan.* 1711, impowering the Waywode *Traurnicht*, to do still more; his own Words are as follow: " I have heard by *Cossacs* and
" *Dworanes* from *Jakutzk*, that you intend to send a Party of *Cossacs*
" and Volunteers to the New Country, or Island, opposite the Mouth of
" the River *Kolyma*; but that you hesitated about doing it without Or-
" ders; therefore I have found it necessary to tell you, that you should
" by no Means neglect to do it; and if other Islands may be discovered,
" you will be pleased to do the same with respect to them. But above
" all Things, the Expedition is to be made this present Year, 1711.
" This I write to you, by Order of His *Czarish* Majesty.
" *Knjas Matfei Gagarin*. *Jan.* 28, 1711."

Hereupon the Waywode *Traurnicht*, prepared for two Expeditions, one to the Mouth of the River *Jana*, and the other to the River *Kolyma*, in Order to go in Search of the pretended Island from both Places at

---

* *Jukagiri, Jukagri,* or *Jukairi* is a Pagan Nation, near the Frozen Sea, between the Mouth of the River *Lena*, and the Promontory of *Talin*, otherwise called *Swjatoi Noss*. The Speech of these People were like the Gabbling of Geese. *Forbisher*, in his Travels, says the same of three Savages, which was brought away from *Davis*'s Streights; *viz.* That they made such a Gabbling and uttered nothing but inarticulate Sounds, except these two Words, *Oxa i ulcho*. These *Jukagiri* hang their Dead on Trees, but the Skeletons, or Bones of their Parents and Relations, they afterwards carry along with them, when they go a Hunting. This agrees with what is affirmed of the *Samojeds* who never bury the Bones of their Parents.

(xvii)

once; for which Purpose, the Men were either to sail by Sea, or to travel over the Ice, till a sufficient Certainty could be obtained, whether there was, or not any such Island.

Concerning the first Expedition, which had *Merkurei Wagin*, a *Cossac*, for its Conductor, I have found several Writings in the Archieves at *Jakutzk*; but they must be judiciously examined, and we must not take every Thing they contain for Truth. *Wagin* departed from *Jakutzk* in Autumn 1711, with eleven other *Cossacs*; and in *May* 1712, he made a Voyage from *Ust-Janskoe Simowie* to the Frozen Sea. The above-mentioned *Jacob Permakow* served him for a Guide. The Carriage consisted, according to the Custom of the Country, of Nartes, a Kind of Sledges, drawn by Dogs. Having followed the Coast to *Swiatoi Noss*, they from thence entered the Sea directly towards the North, and sailed to a desart Island, without Wood, that was from nine to twelve Days Journey in Circumference. From this Island it is said they saw, farther in the Sea, another great Island or Land; but *Wagin* durst not go over to it, as the Spring was too far advanced, and on Account of his wanting Provisions; he therefore returned to the Continent, to provide himself with a sufficient Supply of Fish during the Summer, and to make the Voyage once more the following Winter.

The Place where he reached the Continent on his Return, was between *Swiatoi Noss* and the River *Chroma*, and was called after a *Jakutzk Cossac* who had formerly erected a Cross there, *Kataiew Krest*: From thence he wanted to go to the river *Chroma*, in order to catch Fish; but on their Way he and his Company were in such extreme Want of Provisions, that at first they eat the Dogs which drew their Sledges, and afterwards Mice and other unclean Animals. In this Distress, thinking it too far to the *Chroma*, they returned to the Sea Coast; where they remained the whole Summer, living sparingly upon a few Fishes, Wild-Ducks, Geese, and their Eggs.

In the mean-while, the Remembrance of the Hunger they had suffered, and perhaps the Fear of being in still more miserable Circumstances by going in Search of the Land they had seen, imbittered the Minds of the *Cossacs* that were sent with *Wagin* for *Jakutzk*, against him and the Guide, in such a Manner, that they murdered him, his Son, the *Cossac*. *Jacob Permakow*, and a *Promyschlenoi*. The Fact was discovered by an Accomplice, and the Murderers seized. At their Trial, it appeared that the Guide *Jacob Permakow*, did not take that great Island which they believed to have seen from the first, to be really an Island, but that he thought it no more than Vapours arising from

c the

the Sea. Perhaps Doubts of some Moment may likewise be raised against the Reality of the first Island.

The second Expedition from the River *Kolyma* was just as fruitless as this. It was to have been carried on by 50 Men, in two Vessels; but there were only 22 Men, who sailed in one Vessel, and were conducted by a *Cossac* named *Wasilei Staduchin*, who observed no more than a Promontory, running East from the River *Kolyma* into the Sea; being surrounded by firm Ice, through which no Vessel was able to pass. No Island was to be seen, even at a Distance. They used in this Voyage a Kind of Boats, the Boards of which were fastened, or, in a Manner, sewed together, with Straps, and, from their Construction, have the Name *Schitiki*; they are usually five Fathoms long and two broad, with one Deck, and a flat Bottom caulked with Moss: They are properly made Use of in the Rivers, and in passing to them along the Coasts. The Sail consists of soft Rein Deer Skins, dressed, and instead of Ropes they make Use of Straps of Elk-Skins; the Anchors are of Wood, to which are fastened great Stones. Such a Vessel *Staduchin* had; what Wonder is there, then, that he could make no Discoveries?

In the Year 1714 a new Expedition was prepared from *Jakutzk*, for the same Place, under the Command of *Alexei Markow*, who was to sail from the Mouth of the *Jana*; and if the *Schitiki* were not fit for Sea Voyages, he was to construct, at a proper Place, Vessels fit for prosecuting the Discoveries without Danger. Each Vessel was allowed a Sailor who had been sent by the Governor *Knjas Gagarin* to *Jakutzk*, in order to discover the Navigation from *Ochozk* to *Kamtschatka*.

Markow and his Company were scarce arrived at *Ust-Janskoe Simowie*, when he sent an Account, dated *Feb*. 2, 1715, to the Chancery of *Jakutzk*, mentioning, that it was impossible to navigate the Sea, as it was continually frozen, both in Summer and Winter; and therefore the prescribed Expedition was no otherwise to be carried on but with Sledges drawn by Dogs. In this Manner, he set out, with nine Persons, on the 10th of *March* the same Year, and arrived on the 3d of *April* at *Ust-Janskoe Simowie*. His Account is as follows: That he went seven Days, as fast as his Dogs could draw him (which, in good Ways and Weather, is 80 or 100 Werst in a Day) directly towards the North, on the Sea upon the Ice, without discovering any Land or Island: That it had not been possible for him to get any farther, the Ice rising there in the Sea like Mountains: That he had climbed to the Top of some of them, and looked at a Distance round about, but could discern no Land. At last, wanting Food for his Dogs, many of them died.

Now

Now nothing farther was done, till, in 1723, a Sin-bojarſkoi of *Jakutzk*, whoſe Name was *Fedot Amoſſow*, renewed the old Report of an Iſland in the Frozen Sea, and offered to go thither, and render tributary its Inhabitants. According to him, the Iſland extended from the Mouth of the *Jana* beyond the Mouth of the *Indigirka*. He was ſent with a Party of *Coſſacs*; but he went to the River *Kolyma* to diſcover the Iſland from thence. On *July* 13, 1724, he intended to ſet ſail from the Mouth of this River, but found, according to his Account, ſuch Shoals of Ice before him, that he was hindered in his free Navigation.

Amoſſow ſailed along the Coaſt, eaſtwards, to the Habitations of *Kopai*; which he reached on the 7th of *Auguſt* the ſame Year. He could hardly get along the Coaſt on Account of the Ice; and the Wind being moſtly contrary, he was obliged to lay aſide the Hopes of making Diſcoveries, and to haſte back to the *Kolyma*. As I knew this Man at *Jakutzk*, I have learnt from him, that the Habitations of *Kopai* were about 200 Werſts diſtant, to the eaſtward of the Mouth of the *Kolyma*. He alſo made mention of a ſmall Iſland ſituated very near the Continent; and at the Beginning of the following Winter he made a Journey, with Sledges; of which he gave the following Account to the Chancery of *Jakutzk*: That on the 3d of *November*, 1724, he ſet out from *Niſchnoe Kolymſkoe Simowie*, and met with Land in the Frozen Sea, from whence he came back to *Kolyma* on the 23d of the ſame Month. Upon this Land he ſaw nothing but old Huts covered with Earth; but it was unknown by what People they were inhabited, and where they were gone. The Want of Proviſions, and eſpecially of Food for the Dogs, had obliged him to turn back, without making any farther Diſcoveries. This Journey was very difficult, on Account of the Shoals of Ice, which extended to a great Height, and the Sea Salt with which all the Ice was covered.

To this Account I may add ſome Explanations, which I got by Word of Mouth from *Amoſſow*, at *Jakutzk*. The Place where he left the Continent to go over to the Land, he ſays, is between the Rivers *Tſchukotſchia* and *Alaſea*; it was an Iſland that might be encompaſſed, in a Sledge drawn by Dogs, in a Day, and that it was ſituated about the ſame Diſtance from the Continent; from whence it might be ſeen, on Account of its high rocky Mountains. Behind it there were two other Iſlands, as mountainous as this, ſeparated by narrow Streights, on which he had not been, and conſequently did not know their Extent. The firſt Iſland was without Foreſts; and of Animals he had obſerved no other Footſteps but thoſe of the Rein Deer, whoſe uſual Food is Moſs. The old Huts were built of Wood driven aſhore by the Sea, and covered with Earth. If this be Fact, then it seems that the former Inhabitants were *Jukagiri* or *Tschuktschi*, who, on the Conquest of the Regions about the *Indigirka, Alasea,* and *Kolyma,* fled over thither, and afterwards fought the Continent again.

What has been alledged may, or may not be sufficient to put the Certainty of the pretended Island in the Frozen Sea out of Doubt; yet no farther Researches have been made about it. I cannot deny, that *Amossow*'s written Account, as well as his verbal Relation of it, has not satisfied me; for having Reason to suspect, that it was not so much the Design of making new Discoveries in such dismal Parts, as other self-interested Reasons, that occasioned his offering to undertake this Expedition; that it proceeded from his Desire of becoming a Commander, with which several Advantages are connected; or to trade with the Nations in those Parts, and by this Means revive the Report of the Island in the Frozen Sea. Yet we may suppose, that he afterwards found it necessary to put his written Accounts and verbal Relations in such Order, as to prevent his meeting with Reproach; but if this be the Case, it may farther be asked, Why he did not, in the Beginning of his Account of the Expedition to *Jakutzk,* give an exact Description of the Way he went to the Island, of its Extent, and all other Circumstances? And why he did not, at that Time, make Mention of the other two Islands situated behind the first? One might likewise ask, How it could be possible that *Amossow*'s Island, lying so near the Continent, should not have been discovered in former Voyages to the River *Kolyma,* of which I have found so many circumstantial Accounts in the Archives of *Jakutzk.* At least its small Circumference, according to *Amossow,* does not afford a Confirmation of the old Report, of a large Country extending from the Mouth of the River *Lena,* or *Jana,* as far as opposite the River *Kolyma,* or still farther.

Considering all these Circumstances, it cannot be considered but as too precipitate, when Mess. *De Lisle* and *Buache,* in their new Maps of the Discoveries of *Kamtschatka,* published at *Paris,* represent, under the 73d Degree of North Latitude, an Island opposite the Mouth of the River *Kolyma*; and beyond it, under the 75th Degree, a large Country, said to have been discovered by the *Russians* in 1723. They refer, in this Respect, to written Accounts received by M. *De Lisle* at *St. Petersbourg,* and especially to a Map made by Col. *Schestakow,* a *Cossac*. They alledge historical Circumstances; that, in the first Island, a *Schelagan* Prince, called *Kopai,* was made Prisoner of War, who was the Conductor of the Discovery of the great Country: But this is the very Thing which shews the little Ground there is for these Allegations;

for

(xxi)

for it is not to be supposed, that the Writings of the Archives I have quoted will be called in Question, as they may serve for the best Explanation that can be given. *Kopai*, who did not live upon an Island, but on the Continent, was never a Prisoner to the *Russians*: He for the first Time paid Tribute to *Willegin* the *Promyschelenoi*, for *Russia*; and he did the same in 1724 to *Amossow*: But soon after he deserted the *Russian* Party, and killed some of *Amossow*'s Company. This is all that is known of him. According to the verbal Deposition of *Amossow*, there was situated, not far from his Habitations, a little Island near the Continent. Is it not, then, sufficiently clear, that it is this, and no other Island, which *Scheftakow*, and after him Mess. *De Lisle* and *Buache*, have placed opposite the River *Kolyma*?

As to *Scheftakow*, and his Map, it is to be observed, he could neither read or write, and merely from his Memory, or from the Accounts he had heard from others who could scarcely write, got the Situation of the Countries and Rivers marked upon Maps. He was in 1726 at *St. Petersbourg*, where he formed great Projects for subduing the savage *Tschuktschi*. At that Time several of his Maps appeared, and I myself have received one of them; but never ventured to make Use of it, except in what was confirmed by more certain Accounts. According to this Map, *Kopai*'s Island, as it is marked in Writing, is situated two Days Voyage from the Continent, and takes up almost as much Room in Length as the opposite Coast between the Rivers *Alaseia* and *Kolyma*. It is farther mentioned, that it is inhabited by a resolute People called the *Schelages*. Behind it, to the North, there is a Coast, under the Name of the *Large Country*, between which, and the Island, it is said in express Words, that is not quite two Days Voyage from the Island. This being founded neither on verbal or written Accounts, may justly be considered as an Addition by *Scheftakow*, to what he had had from others. So that I cannot see what can be taken from this, more than from the other Reports, to fix the Situation of this Land, though we suppose its Reality to be out of the Question.

But what shall we say, when, according to the Testimony of *P. Avril*, who, in 1686, pretends to have heard at *Smolensk*, that that Country is inhabited, and full of Forests. I think this is plainly contrary to Fact, if the former Discoveries are to be depended upon; and if we consider, that along the Coasts of the Frozen Sea there are no Forests, and that these northerly Regions admit of none. In the mean while, the Supposition given in Writing by *P. Avril*, to the Waywode of *Smolensk*, that by means of this Island *America* was peopled from *Asia*, does honour to those Times, if even the Island itself should be

proved

proved to have no Existence; as it may be understood of the Islands and the Continent opposite *Tschukotskoi Nost*, of which we shall mention what has been discovered in former Times, without the Navigation of *Deschnew*.

Sheftakow's Map is here very imperfect; it only says, "upon the "Noss dwell the stubborn *Tschuktschi*, who throw Stones with Slings. "There are also many red Foxes." And opposite, on the East Side, there is marked a large Island, which is thus described: "An Island op- "posite *Anadirskoi Noss*, well peopled: Upon it are found abundance "of all Sorts of Animals. The Inhabitants are not tributary, and are subject to none." Another Map which I got at *Jakutzk*, from a *Dwo- ranin*, named *Iwan Lwaw*, who is the Author of it, furnishes us with some more Accounts. It represents a two-fold Noss; the farthermost towards the North East, which, from the Nation of the *Tschutschi*, is commonly called *Tschukotskoi Noss*, and has there the Name of *Schelatz- koi*, from the *Schelagen*, who are a particular Race among the *Tschuktschi*. The other, which lies South from this, though it is far enough from the River *Anadir*, is called from that River *Anadiriksi Noss*. It is therefore a Mistake in *Sheftakow*'s Map, to give this last Name to the former, which he has quite forgot. *Tschukotskoi*, or *Schelatzkoi Noss*, is not limited, as the Author of the Map did not know its Extent. In a large Gulph between *Tschukotskoy* and *Anadirskoi Noss* lies an Island, which is said to be inhabited by the *Tschuktschi*, and another over- against *Anadirskoi Noss*, the one farther from the Continent than the other; which are described in the following Manner: "To the first "Island is half a Day's Voyage; upon it lives a People whom the "*Tschuktschi* call *Achjuchaljat*; these speak their own Language, wear "Cloaths of Duck-skins, and live by catching of Sea-Horses and "Whales; and, as the Island is without Forests, they boil their Pro- "visions with Train Oil. The second is two Days Voyage Distance "from the first; the Inhabitants are called, in the *Tschuktschi* "Language, *Peekeli*. They have Teeth set in through their Cheeks; "they live in fortified Places, and are also cloathed with Duck-skins." I am of Opinion, that the Situation here given to this Island is a Mistake, and that it must be looked for over-against *Tschukotskoi Noss*. Beyond this Island there is marked a large Country, the Inhabitants of which are called by the *Tschutkschi*, *Kitschin Eljat*. They have their own Language; wear Cloaths of the Skins of Sables, Foxes, and Rein Deer, dwell in fortified Places, have their Habitations in the Ground, and shoot with Bows and Arrows. All the Animals of whose Skins

(xxiii)

they make Cloaths, are found there. Their Wood is Pine, Fir, Birch, and the Larch Tree.

To this I will add another Map, whose Author is also an Inhabitant of *Jakutzk*, in which *Schelatskoi Nofs* is unlimited, as in the former. Of the Inhabitants it is here said, "That they speak their own Language, "are warlike and cannot be subdued; because, if any one of them is "taken Prisoner, he kills himself." This is in general the Case with respect to the rest of the People of *Siberia*, whose first Subjection was mostly effected by taking some of them Prisoners, and keeping them as Hostages for the Fidelity of the rest; or, as they used to express it in *Siberia*, as *Amanaten*. Over-against *Schelatzkoi Nofs* another unlimited Country presents itself; the Inhabitants of which are called, in the *Tschuktschan* Language, *Kykykmei*, and are said to resemble the *Jukagiri*. Other Accounts which I shall mention here, are founded in the Writings of our Chiefs.

On the 14th of *March* 1710, the Waywode *Dorofei Trauernicht* enquired at *Jakutzk* of several *Coffacs* there, who had been at *Anadirskoi Ostrog*, about all the Circumstances of the *Tschuktschan* Nations, and had from three *Coffacs*, *Timofei Daurzow*, *Fedor Pornoi*, and *Peter Mungal*, the following Relation: In 1701, the Tributary *Jukagiri*, under *Anadirskoi Ostrog* complained to the Commander of the Place, that they were often attacked by the *Tschuktschi*, and desired that some *Ruffians* might be sent with them to subdue these Enemies. The Commander gave them Twenty-four Men, who were joined by 110 *Jukagiri*, who were eight Weeks in their March from *April* to *June*.

The first Action was to summon, on the Sea Coast of *Anadir*, thirteen Habitations of the *Tschuktschi*, to submit themselves and pay Tribute; but this they refused, and an Engagement ensuing, about ten Men of the *Tschuktschoi* were killed, and the Women and Children made Prisoners. The Men whom they thought to keep as Prisoners, soon after killed each other; but some escaped, and raised near 300 Men at *Tschukotskoi Nofs*, who ventured to make head against the *Ruffians* and *Jukagiri*, but were defeated, near 200 being left dead on the Spot, and the rest ran away. The next Day, an Army of above 3000 *Tschuktschi* was seen on their March: The Battle began in the Morning and lasted till the Evening; in which many of the *Tschuktschi* were slain; and yet the *Ruffians* and *Jukagiri* lost no Men, and had only ten wounded: but the *Tschuktschi* retired, and encamped in such a Manner, that the *Ruffians* and *Jukagiri* were surrounded by them for five Days: At last, however, they escaped, and retired to *Anadirskoi*, without Loss. Upon this Occasion, the following Observation has been made:

made: Although it is not to be denied that the *Tschuktschi* are expert at throwing Stones with Slings, yet in War they mostly make use of Bows and Arrows. The *Tschukotskoi Nos* is quite destitute of all Wood: Those of the *Tschuktschi*, who keep tame Rein Deer, live by them; but those who walk on foot, live by catching Sea-horses, Whales, and other Fish. In the midst of the Nos, between the rocky Mountains, dwell the *Tschuktschi*, who keep Rein Deer; but the Footmen live on both Sides on the Sea Coast. There are no Sables on the Nos, and no other wild Animals, except red Foxes and Rein Deer. Sea-horse Teeth are found in Abundance on the Coast.

Thus far the written Relation taken down at *Jakutzk*. A *Pietidesatnik* of the *Cossacs*, called *Matsei Skrebykin*, who at that Time was sent as Commander to *Anadirskoi Ostrog*, received Orders to get better Intelligence in relation to the *Tschuktschi*, and the Country inhabited by them. This was done; and the following Account is the Fruit of his Endeavours:

 "*Anadirsk*, Sept. 2, 1711. The Deposition of the *Jakutzich*, Cos-
" sac Peter Iliin Sin *Popow*, of the *Promischlenoi*, *Jegar Wasiliew Sin*
" *Toldin*, and the newly baptized *Jukagir Iwan Wasiliew Sin Tereschkin*.
" *Peter Iliin Sin Popow*, was sent with two others, who served him as
" Interpreters, on the 13th of *January*, 1711, by the Governor *Fedor*
" *Kotkowskoi*, to the Banks of the River *Anadir*, to receive the Tri-
" bute from some tributary *Tschuktschi*; whereupon they were ordered
" to go to the Nos to admonish the obstinate *Tschuktschi* to pay Obe-
" dience; to receive Hostages from them; to get full Intelligence con-
" cerning their Manner of Living, their Customs, and the Nature
" of the Country and the neighbouring Islands; and then to return to
" *Anadirskoy Ostrog*. *Popow* went from the Mouth of the River *Anadir*
" to the *Tschuktschi*, who lived beyond a Gulph, and from thence to
" *Tschukotskoi Nos*. He every where met with a Denial with respect
" to their rendering themselves subject, and paying Tribute. The
" *Tschuktschi* said, that, formerly, *Russians* came to them in Kotsches
" by Sea, to whom they paid no Tribute, and therefore they would
" not do it now; consequently, he ought to expect no Hostages from
" them. However, he had an Opportunity to make many useful Ob-
" servations, and to get such Intelligence as were agreeable to his
" Orders. The solemn Obligation, or Oath of *Tschuktschi*, consists in
" calling on the Sun to be Security for their Promises. The *Tschuktschi*
" who dwell on the Nos keep tame Rein Deer, on Account of which they
" often change their Habitations between the Rocks; those who have no
" Rein Deer live on both Sides of the Nos, on the Banks of the Sea,
" where

" where the Sea Horses are used to come on Shore. They have im-
" moveable Huts, which they dig in the Ground, or cover with Earth.
" Both live by hunting wild Rein Deer, catching Whales, Sea Horses,
" Seals, &c. and upon Roots and Herbs. Opposite the Noss on both
" Sides, as well in the Sea of *Kolyma*, as in *Anadir*, an Island is said
" to be seen at a great Distance, which the *Tschuktschi* call a large
" Country, and say, that People dwell there who have large Teeth put
" into their Mouths that project thro' their Cheeks. These People
" are different in their Language, and Manner of Living, from the
" *Tschuktschi*, who have waged War against them Time out of Mind.
" Their Weapons are, like those of the latter, Bows and Arrows.
" *Popow* found ten Men of these People disfigured with their projecting
" Teeth; these were Prisoners of War among the *Tschuktschi*; and
" he observed, that the Teeth, thus set in, were cut from those of
" the Sea-horse. In Summer Time they sail, in one Day, to the
" Land, in Baidares, a Sort of Vessels constructed with Whale-
" bones, and covered with Seal-skins; and in Winter Time, going
" swift with Rein Deer, the Journey may likewise be made in a
" Day. As on the Noss there are no other Animals but Foxes and
" Wolves, and even these are scarce for Want of Wood, so on
" the other Land are found all Sorts of Beasts, as Sables, several
" Sorts of Foxes, Wolves, white Bears, Sea Otters, &c. The In-
" habitants keep large Herds of tame Rein Deer: they live by
" catching of Sea Animals, and live likewise on Berries, Roots, and
" Herbs. They are, like the *Tschuktschi*, without any Governors.
" Their Wood is Cedar, Fir, several Sorts of Pines, and the Larch
" Tree; which Kinds of Wood *Popow* observed in the Baidares
" and Huts of the *Tschuktschi*. According to the Computation of
" *Popow*, in relation to the Number of these People that live on
" the Noss, as well of those that have Rein Deer, as of those that
" are without, they are about 2000 Men, or more; whereas the
" Islanders are said to be three Times that Number; which is con-
" firmed, not only by the Prisoners, but by one of the *Tschuktschi*,
" who has often been there. From *Anadirsko Ostrog* to the Noss they
" go with loaden Rein Deer, and consequently pretty slow, in ten
" Weeks, and even then they must not be detained on the Roads by
" violent Winds, which are generally accompanied with Snow. The
" Way leads by a Rock called *Matkol*, situated in the middlemost or
" deepest Part of a great Bay."

d

(xxvi)

To this I will add another Relation, received from some *Tschuktschi* at the Time of their coming to *Anadirskoi Oſtrog*, in order to acknowledge the Dominion of the *Ruſſians*.

"The ſolemn Obligation, or Oath, with the *Tſchuktſchi*, is, by
" conſtituting the Sun, or their Sorcerer-Prieſts, their Sureties. They live
" on the Noſs, beyond the Rivers *Anadir* and *Kolyma*; their Number
" may be between 3 or 4000, and upwards, they themſelves do not
" know exactly how ſtrong they are, ſince they have but little Know-
" ledge of Numbers. As they live without Government, every one
" does what he pleaſes; however, thoſe who belong to one Tribe
" keep together. Their Herds of tame Rein Deer are numerous; by
" them they live, and, in the mean-while, they catch wild Rein Deer,
" Sea-horſes, Whales, and other Sea Animals, which ſerve them for
" Food. Of wild land Animals there are none upon the Noſs but
" Foxes and Wolves; Sables are not found there, becauſe there are no
" Woods. The Noſs is full of rocky Mountains, and the low Grounds
" conſiſt of Land covered with Turf. Oppoſite to it lies an Iſland,
" within Sight of it, of no great Extent, and void of Wood. It is
" inhabited by People who have the ſame Aſpect as the *Tſchuktſchi*,
" but are a quite different Nation, and ſpeak their own Language,
" though they are not numerous. It is half a Day's Voyage, with
" Badaires from the Noſs to the Iſland. There are no Sables on the
" Iſland, and no other Animals but Foxes, Wolves, and Rein Deer.
" Beyond the Iſland is a large Continent that can be ſcarcely diſ-
" cerned from it, and that only in clear Days; in calm Weather one
" may row over the Sea from the Iſland to the Continent, which is in-
" habited by a People who in every particular reſemble the *Tſchutkſchi*.
" There are large Foreſts of Fir, Pine, Larch, and Cedar Trees;
" great Rivers flow through the Country, and fall into the Sea. The
" Inhabitants have Dwellings and fortified Places of Abode, environed
" with Ramparts of Earth; they live upon wild Rein Deer and Fiſh;
" their Cloaths are made of Sable, Fox, and Rein Deer Skins, for
" Sables and Foxes are there in great Abundance. The Number of
" Men in that Country may be twice or three Times as many as
" that of the *Tſchuktſchi*, who are often at War with them." *Thus far this Relation deſerves Credit; but now follows ſomething fabulous.*
" There are likewiſe ſaid to be People in this Country who have Tails
" like Dogs; ſpeak their own Language; are often at War among
" themſelves, and are without Religion: They wear Cloaths like the
" former, and live upon wild Rein Deer and Sea Animals. Another
" Nation there, is ſaid to have Feet like Ravens, covered with the ſame
" Kind

" Kind of Skins as theirs. They never wear Shoes or Stockings."
We shall be so just as to excuse the Fables of the wild *Tschuktschi*, since
European Authors, writing of unknown Countries, have fallen into no
less Absurdities.

The rest of the Relation regards, in the first Place, the Distance
between *Tschukotskoi Noss* and the Mouth of the River *Anadir*: To determine which, the *Tschuktschi* said, " That they spent three Weeks,
" or less Time, in sailing with their Baideres from the inner Bay of the
" *Anadir* along the Coast, to the Extremity of the Noss, over-against
" which the Island lies." A Circumstance next occurs, which we
should entirely omit, as foreign to our Purpose, if it did not contain a very particular Custom of the *Tschuktschi*, so contrary to the
Customs of all civilized Nations, that, though Something of it *is*
mentioned in Mr. Resident *Weber*'s *Russia Changed* *, yet, without
farther Confirmation, is hardly to be credited. What M. *Paulus
Venetus* relates † of the Hospitality of the Inhabitants of the Country
of *Camul*, and what is observed of *Tibet* ‡; what *Witsen* ‖, and the
Jesuit *Trigaut* repeats after him; and what this latter § alledges about the
Land of *Caschemir*, is, out of all Doubt, the same with the *Tschuktschi*:
" When a Stranger comes to them, let him be of their own, or another
" Nation, they offer him, upon the first Salutation, their Wives and
" Daughters, as Bedfellows. If they are not handsome enough, or
" are too old for the Guest, they bring him some from among their
" Neighbours; whereupon the Woman presents him a Bason of Urine,
" fresh made in his Presence, with which he is obliged to rince his
" Mouth: If he refuses the Offer, they hold him for their Enemy;
" but, from his accepting of it, they conclude his sincere Friendship."
This the *Tschuktschi* told, not only at *Anadirk*, but it is contained in
the written Account I have given; and I have also frequently heard it
at *Jakutzk*, by People who have been amongst the *Tschuktschi*.

We shall not amuse ourselves with comparing these Accounts where
they contradict each other; the Difference only consists in things of no
Moment. The chief Point still remains the same, that there is a real
Separation between the two Parts of the World, *Asia*, and *America*;
that it consists only in a narrow Streight; and that, within this Streight,
one or more Islands are situated; by which the Passage from one of
these Parts of the World to the other is facilitated. From antient
Times the Inhabitants of each of these Parts of the World had Knowledge of each other. Other Accounts from these Parts though I cannot

* Vol. i. p. 406.   † Book i. Ch. 46.   ‡ Book ii. Ch. 37.   ‖ North
and East *Tartary*. Edit. ii. Pag. 234, 235.   § Pag. 341.

prove

prove them by written Originals, like those hitherto alledged, yet they do not seem to me unworthy of Attention. People must believe me upon my Word, and give Credit to me when I assert, that they have been told me at *Jakutsk* by Persons of Credit.

What *Nikifor Malgin* says above, of bearded People on an Island in the *Penschinskan Sea*, and which I have interpreted of the *Kuriles*, this the Inhabitants of *Anadirskoi Ostrog* say of the Continent, which lies over-against the Habitations of the *Tschuktschi*. There is said to live somewhere in that Country, a People who have a great deal in common with the *Russians*, not only in respect to Beards and Cloathing, but likewise in their Trades and Employments: The *Tschuktschi* get Platters and other wooden Vessels from them, that are hardly to be distinguished from those made in *Russia*. Some believe that they are really descended from the *Russians*, and that their Ancestors were driven by Shipwreck to this Country, where they have remained.

It is said, that in the Year 1715, there lived a Man of a foreign Nation at *Kamtschatka*, who, upon Account of the *Kamtschatkan* cedar Nuts, and the low Shrubs on which they grow, said, that he came from a Country where there were larger Cedars, which bore bigger Cedar Nuts than those of *Kamtschatka*; that his Country was situated to the East of *Kamtschatka*; that there were found in it great Rivers, which discharged themselves westward into the *Kamtschatkan* Sea; that the Inhabitants called themselves *Tontoli*; they resembled, in their Manner of Living, the People of *Kamtschatka*, and made Use of Leathern Boats, or Baidares, like the *Kamtschadales*: That, many Years ago, he went over, with some more of his Countrymen, to *Karaginskoi Ostrow*, where his Companions were slain by the Inhabitants, and he alone made his Escape to *Kamtschatka*.

On *Karaginsko Ostrow*, an Island opposite the River *Karaga*, by which it is called, it is said, in the subterraneous Dwellings of the Inhabitants, there are observed great Beams of Pine and Fir Trees, with which these Caves are partly wainscotted: The Inhabitants being asked whence they had these Beams, since such Kind of Wood was not found in *Kamtschatka*, or the neighbouring Islands? They made Answer, that, sometimes, they were driven on Shore by easterly Winds, when, for Want of Wood in the Island, they used to take them and make Use of them.

It has ever been observed in *Kamtschatka*, that, in Winter Time, a strong East Wind drives Ice to the *Kamtschatkan* Coast in two or three Days, and then certain Birds annually fly from the East, which having remained some Months on the Coasts of *Kamtschatka*, return back. What else can be concluded from this, but that

the

(xxix)

the Continent opposite the Country of the *Tschuktschi* extends southward of *Kamtschatka*? and may not this be likewise conjectured from the Martins found in that Country, which are not to be met with even in the northernmost Countries, nor in *Siberia*, except in the Dominions about *Catherinebourg* and the *Isettischen Province*. Perhaps in the former Relations of the neighbouring Continent, instead of Sables, are to be understood Martins: This is certain, that the *Tschuktschi* get Cloaths of Martins Skins from thence: Some such have now and then been brought from *Anadirskoi Ostrog* to *Jakutzk*; as is known to every Person thereabouts.

'Tis probable, that here, by the Continent situated eastward, near *Kamtschatka* and the Country of the *Tschuktschi*, is to be understood, not a large Island, but *North America* itself; since its Nature, so far as it is known, gives Reason for this Supposition. *French* Travellers who have been in *Louisiana* make mention of a great River that flows westward, to the Sea, from the Head of the *Missouri*, which empties itself into the *Missisippi*: 'Tis true, they have not been on that River; but 'tis enough that they have Intelligence of it from the Heathen Nations who live there. The *Missouri* falls into the *Missisippi* between the 39th and 40th Degree North Latitude, and is reckoned four hundred Leagues and upwards to the Middle of the Course of the *Missouri*, and, from thence, six Days Journey to that River; which, according to the Account of the People there, falls into the unknown Westerly Ocean*. Although Mess. *De Lisle* and *Buache*, in the Maps they have lately published, represent this Sea as a great Lake, or Gulph, situated between the 40th and 50th Degree of North Latitude; but the Ground on which they support their Opinion does not seem to me of sufficient Weight. *William De Lisle*, the Royal Geographer, figured to himself, first, the Situation of the Western Ocean in this Manner, in the Year 1697; following in this the Descriptions of Journeys in which were contained the Depositions of *Americans* about this Sea, and the Rivers falling into it. In the Year 1700 he composed a Book on this Subject, in Hopes of animating the *French* Ministry to make Preparations for new Discoveries. But when we come to a close Examination of the Testimonies alledged therein, we find that the greatest Part of them do not speak of a Sea or Gulph, but of the Atlantic Ocean itself; that the

* We will take the latest Testimony: Memoire sur la Louisiane, par M. Le Sage du Pratz in *Journal Oeconomique*, 1751, *Sept*. P. 140. On croit que le Missouri vient de l'Ouest. Selon le Rapport des Peuples du païs; il a 800 lieuеs de cours, & à six Journées au Nord du milieu de son cours ontrouve une autre riviere, qui contant du levant au couchant va se se jetter dans *la mer inconnue de l'Ouest*.

(xxx)

rest are doubtful; but all of them are of such a Nature, that an Opinion, which has sufficient Grounds against it, cannot be confirmed by them. Let us look in the Map of *America*. The River *Missouri* falls into the *Missisippi* somewhat below the 40th Degree of North Latitude; we will suppose it flows from the North-West, as the People in those Parts alledge: From its Mouth to its Head it is reckoned 800 *French* Leagues: How does that consist with the Western Sea, in the Manner Mess. *De Lisle* and *Buache* figure it to themselves? For here this Western Sea or Gulph, which they believe takes up the same Parts which the River *Missouri* ought to pass through; but it is still six Days Journey from the River *Missouri* to the River that falls into the Western Sea. This River is of considerable Bigness, consequently its Head must be very remote; but Mess. *De Lisle* and *Buache* represent it as quite narrow and short, probably from no other Reason but to have sufficient Room for their Western Sea. They add to the Arguments of M. *De Lisle*, sen. the Travels of *John de Fuca*, which we have shewn above cannot be relied on; and when M. *Buache* endeavours to confirm his Opinion by the Testimonies of modern Travellers of the present Century, we may easily see that it is by that Means only the more weakened [*]. We may subjoin to this, that the *Americans* call the Western Sea *an unknown Sea*, *i. e.* such a one, the Bounds or Limits of which they neither know, nor can know; but was it a Sea or Gulph, on all Sides surrounded with Land, how should the People who live near it be unable to give better Accounts of it? Therefore, in my Opinion, the westerly River, so often mentioned, falls into the *Atlantic* Ocean, either opposite *Kamtschatka*, or over-against the Country of the *Tschuktschi*; so that, hereby, the Accounts received from the *Tschuktschi* are confirmed, and with these we must content ourselves, till something more precise happens to be known of those Parts by more exact Discoveries.

We proceed now to the Islands situated towards the South from *Kamtschatka*, the Discovery of which we shall likewise consider, as it has been made gradually, and so far as the proposed Period of Time has a Share in it.

The Country of *Kamtschatka* has been known at *Jakutzk* ever since the Year 1690; but only from a mere Report. Hence it is that *Ifbrand Ides*, in his Travels to *China*, Chap. xx. and in his Map belonging to that Work, was able to mention it. The first Expedition

---

[*] New Charts of the Discoveries of Admiral *Fonte*, and other Navigators, &c. with their Explications, &c. by M. *De Lisle*, printed at *Paris* in 1753, 4to. Geographical and Physical Considerations on the new Discoveries, &c. by M. *Buache*. *Paris* 1753, 4to.

to

to it was made by sixteen *Jakutzk Cossacs* in 1696, whose Leader was called *Lucas Semoenow Sin Morosko*, in which they did not quite reach the River *Kamtschatka*, but were content to receive Tribute from a *Kamtschedale Ostrog*, and to return with it to *Anadirskoi Ostrog*, from whence these *Cossacs* were dispatched. The Piatidesiatnik *Wolodimer Atlassow*, who is commonly represented as the Discoverer of *Kamtschatka*, was at that Time Commander at *Anadirskoi Ostrog:* He had sent *Morosko* to the *Korjakin* on the River *Opuka*, to make them tributary; the rest *Morosko* did without Orders. *Atlassow* writes of him, that he came within four Days Voyage of the River *Kamtschatka*, and with this agrees a verbal Tradition, that terminates his Voyage at the River *Tigil*. *Morosko*, on the contrary, mentions, that he had been only one Day's Voyage distant from the River *Kamtschatka*. In the *Kamtschedale Ostrog* he found unknown Writings, which he brought back with him. We shall prove that they were *Japanese*; for when *Atlassow*, the succeeding Year, followed the Steps of *Morosko*, with a more numerous Company, by erecting a Cross *, took Possession of the River *Kamtschatka*, at the Place where the River *Kanutsch* falls into it, and founded a Simowie in the Parts where afterwards *Werchnei Kamtschatkoi Ostrog* was built, he met on the River *Itscha* a *Japanese*, who two Years before had been cast by Shipwreck on the Coast of *Kamtschatka*, at the Place where the River *Opala* empties itself into the Sea, on the South of *Bolschaia Reka*.

The Intelligence of *Atlassow*'s Voyage, which *Strahlenberg* has subjoined at the End of his Description, is a Relation, by which he probably answered many Questions that were put to him, and which, to all Appearance, were taken down in Writing at *Moscow*. It is no Deposition before a Magistrate, and does not agree with that which *Atlassow* mentions in a Petition, after his Arrival at *Jakutzk* in the Year 1700; nor with that which he deposited at *Moscow*, in the *Siberian* Prikase, in 1701; it seems rather to have been set down by some inquisitive private Person; wherefore it is much more circumstantial than the other; and as *Atlassow* may have been asked about more Things than he knew, and yet he unwilling to pass for ignorant, some false Circumstances in Relation to the Country may have arisen from it, or, to judge with greater Candour, from a Defect in his Memory. Others are manifestly owing to a Misunderstanding of the Writer, or, perhaps, of the Translator. In *Strahlenberg*'s Relation, the *Japanese* whom *Atlassow*

---

* The Cross was still seen at the Time of the last *Kamtschatkan* Expedition, and had the following Inscription: *On the 13th of July, in the Year 1205,* [This Date is from *German* Copy; but the Editor thinks it should be 1697] *this Cross was erected, by* Piatdesiatnick Wolodimir Atlassow, *and his Company, consisting of 55 Men.*

found

found in *Kamtschatka* is called an *Indian*; and in the Remarks it is said, that he was a *Japanese*, who afterwards was brought to *Moscow* when the *Swedes* were in *Siberia*. This *Japanese* seems to have been confounded with another, who will be mentioned hereafter. *Atlassow* himself, in his Petition, has called the Stranger a Prisoner from the Kingdom of *Osacka*. What else can here be understood, but the great trading Town of *Osacka* in *Japan*? *Atlassow* took him with him in his Voyage to *Jakutzk*; but it does not appear that he arrived there. *Strahlenberg*'s Intelligence says, that on Account of Weakness he staid behind at *Anadirsk*.

These Intelligences also contain something of the Islands situated to the South of the Country of *Kamtschatska*. We call them the *Kurilian* Islands, because several of them are inhabited by the *Kuriles*. The People in that Country are said to have told *Atlassow*, that they contained walled Towns; but what Sort of People dwelt in them nobody could tell. *Strahlenberg* here remarks, that the northerly *Japanese* Islands are here meant; and indeed, since the Islands situated in the Neighbourhood of *Kamtschatka* have no such Towns, it seems that this Circumstance must have its Rise from the said *Japanese*. What is pretended of a Continental Commerce between these *Japanese* Islands and the Country of *Kamtschatka*, has been found without Foundation in later Times. All Commerce from *Japan*, towards the North, is confined to a few of the neighbouring Islands, or to the Land of *Jeso*: Of this the *Japanese* in *Kamtschatka* seems to have spoken: The rest of the Islands, and the Country of *Kamtschatka* itself, were entirely unknown to the *Japanese* who were stranded on *Kamtschatka*, the Winds and Weather having driven them thither against their Will, which we have had several Opportunities of learning, since the following Times have furnished more Instances of *Japanese* Ships stranded on the Coast of *Kamtschatka*. Two Points that were learned from this first *Japanese* were essential: First, That the Kingdom of *Osacka*, as *Atlassow* calls it, or the Land of *Japan*, is not at a very great Distance to the South of *Kamtschatka*: And, secondly, That the intermediate Space at Sea is filled up with several great and small Islands, the Inhabitants whereof, (the *Kuriles*) are called by the *Japanese*, *Jeso*, or *Eso*; out of which the *Europeans* have formed the Name of the Land of *Eso*, or *Jesso*.

Atlassow should have made a second Voyage to *Kamtschatka* in the Year 1702, after his being declared Chief of the *Cossacs*, as a Reward for his Services; but his bad Conduct on his Return to *Jakutzk* brought upon him a severe Scrutiny; on Account of which his second Voyage
thither

thither was commenced no sooner than the Year 1706. During the mean Time, in the Years 1701, 1702, and 1703, the three Oftroges *Werchnei*, *Nifchnei*, and *Bolfcheretfkoi*, were built by other Commanders fent from *Jakutzk* to *Kamtfchatka*; and, in the Year 1706, a Beginning had been made of the Conqueft of the fouthernmoft Part of *Kamtfchatka*: Upon which Occafion the *Ruffian* Nations coming to the Extremity of the Neck of Land, convinced themfelves of the Situation of the neareft *Kurilian* Iflands, by Infpection; though only at a Diftance, and without leaving the Continent. An Infurrection amongft the *Kamtfchedales*, in the Year 1707, in which *Bolfcheretfkoi Oftrog*, with the whole Garrifon there, were loft, was, doubtlefs, the Reafon of their not proceeding with the Difcoveries. On the contrary, a Mutiny of the *Coffacs* againft their Commanders, which, in 1711, coft the *Wolodimir Atlaffow*, and two others, their Lives, ferved for this Purpofe, that the Guilty, in order to atone for their Crime, firft reduced to Obedience the *Kamtfchedales* of *Bolfcheretzkoi*, rebuilt *Boltfcheretzkoi Oftrog*, and from among themfelves provided it with a Garrifon; and, next, were fo affiduous in difcovering the *Kurilian* Iflands, that the Inhabitants of the two firft could hefitate no longer about acknowledging themfelves fubject to the Dominion of the *Ruffians*. In the preceding Year, viz. in *April* 1710, another *Japanefe* Veffel was ftranded on the Coaft of *Kamtfchatka*, in the *Kaligirian* Bay (which lies North of *Awatfcha*) of which ten Perfons came afhore, who were furprized by the *Kamtfchedales* as Enemies, and fix of them made Prifoners, after four had been killed in the Engagement. Of thefe fix Perfons, four again fell into the Hands of the *Ruffians*; one, called *Sanima*, was in 1714 fent to the Imperial Court at *Peterfbourg*, and as they foon learnt fo much of the *Ruffian* Language, as plainly to anfwer the Queftions that were put to them, the Knowledge of the Situation and Nature of the *Kurilian* Iflands was fet in a ftill plainer Light by their Relations, and by what was otherwife learnt from the *Kurilians*. But before we fpeak of this, we muft fee what came to the Knowledge of the *Ruffian Coffacs* from their own Experience, in Relation to the two firft Iflands, in the Year 1711.

Danilo Anzipborow, and *Iwan Kofirewfkoi*, Ringleaders of the *Coffac* Mutiny, had rebuilt *Bolcheretfkoi Oftrog*, and fubdued the *Kamtfchedales* who dwelt in thofe Parts. Hereupon they fet out, on the firft of *Auguft* 1711, with as many Men as they could, without weakening *Bolfcheretfkoi*, and paffed, with fmall Baidares, a Streight, to the firft Ifland; where, at the Mouth of the Rivulet *Kudutugan*, a Multitude of the *Kuriles* ftood affembled, who entered into an Engagement with the

the *Ruſſians*. However, the firſt Iſland is not inhabited by proper *Kuriles*: Theſe are, ſtrictly ſpeaking, the Poſſeſſors of the ſecond and following Iſlands; but it is uſual in *Kamtſchatka* to give the Name of *Kuriles* even to the Inhabitants of the Continent ſouth of *Bolſchaiareka* and *Awatſcha*, though they differ in Dialect from the *Kamtſchedales*. A Lake in the Midſt of the Country is called *Kurilskoe Oſero*, while the *Kamtſchedale Oſtrog*, on an Iſland in this Lake, bears the Name of *Kurilskoi Oſtrog*; and with theſe Inhabitants thoſe of the firſt Iſland, who, perhaps, may, in Part, have fled thither from the Continent ſince the Year 1706, and have formed a new Nation. I follow here written Intelligences, founded on the common Uſe of the Name. The Conſequence of the Engagement was, that the Inhabitants of the Iſland, after loſing ten Men, and having many more wounded, promiſed an eternal Subjection; though no Tribute was received from them immediately; for the Iſland had neither Sables or Foxes, nor did the Otters uſe to make their Appearance in the Sea hereabouts. The Inhabitants lived by catching of Seals, the Skins of which, together with thoſe of Swans, wild Geeſe, and Ducks, ſerved them for Cloathing. As for the Reſt, the *Coſſacs* greatly praiſed theſe People for their Valour in War; and they had not met with any like them in all *Kamtſchatka*. Three *Kurilian* Veſſels, built at the firſt Iſland, was uſed in the Navigation to the ſecond Iſland, which immediately took Place.

On this ſecond Iſland, according to the *Coſſacs*, dwelt a People called *Jeſowitenes*: Theſe aſſembled near a Brook termed *Jaſſowilka*, in great Numbers, and completely armed; therefore the *Coſſacs*, who were but few, and were beſides in Want of Powder, would not venture to engage them; they rather endeavoured, by good Words, to perſuade the Iſlanders to acknowledge themſelves ſubject to *Ruſſia*, and to pay a certain Tribute: But theſe anſwered, "Hitherto we have been ſubject " to nobody, and have known nothing of paying Tribute. Sables and " Foxes are not found amongſt us; but in Winter Time we catch " Beavers, and theſe we have already ſold to Strangers who come to us " from a neighbouring Country, which you ſee lying there towards the " South, and who give for them Iron Tools, Muſlin, and other " Goods; conſequently you have no Tribute to expect now." What they intended to do for the future they did not declare; wherefore the *Coſſacs* found it adviſeable, after ſtaying two Days on this Iſland, to return to the Continent, and arrived, on the 18th of *September*, at *Bolſcheretskoi*. The Name of *Jeſſowitenes*, ſeems to be an Imitation of the Name *Jeſo*; by which the *Kuriles* are called by the *Japaneſe*. As, probably,

probably, this Name came to be known to the *Coffacs* of *Kamtfchatka* by Means of the ftranded *Japanefe*, fo we may conclude that, from this and the fecond Ifland, the Nations of the *Kuriles*, as has been already mentioned, had their real Origin.

After this firſt Attempt, two other Expeditions were made, in 1712 and 1713, from *Kamtfchatka* to the *Kurilian* Iflands, both founded on an Order received from *Jakutzk*. This Order was occafioned by the Inftructions given to the Waywode *Trauernicht*, by the Prince *Wafilei Iwanowitfch Gagarin*, as is mentioned above; in which Inftructions, amongſt the reſt, it is recommended to the Care of the Waywode, to have Enquiry made after the Iflands fituated near *Kamtfchatka*, and a Defcription given of them. Both Expeditions were performed under the Conduct of the *Coffac* named *Iwan Kofirewskoi*, who feems to have been moſt affiduous in getting Intelligence from the fhipwrecked *Japanefe*. *Kofirewskoi*, afterwards, in the Year 1717, turned Monk, and from that Time was called *Ignatei Kofirewſkoi*. He came in 1720 to *Jakutzk*, and in 1730 to *Mofcow*; from whence an Account of his Merit was ſent to *Peterſburgh*, and inferted in the *Peterſburg Gazette* of the 26th of *March*. His whole Life was a Chain of Broils and Difquietudes; but this is not to the Purpofe. His Intelligences, which he delivered in *Kamtfchatka*, to the Commanders there, and afterwards in the Chancery of the Waywode of *Jakutzk*; as alfo to Capt. *Bering*, on his coming to *Jakutzk* in 1726, are altogether remarkable. They were accompanied with a Kind of Draughts, in order to reprefent, in a plainer Manner, the Continent and the Iflands; of all which I will here give an Extract.

Firſt of all, a low Promontory extends from the South End of *Kamtfchatka*, to the Diftance of 15 or 20 Werfts, into the Sea; it is about 400 Fathoms broad; and, on Account of its fquare Figure, is called *Lopatka*, *i. e.* a Shovel.

From this one may row over a Streight with Baidares in two or three Hours, and arrive at the firſt Ifland, *Schumtſchu*, which is inhabited by the *Kuriles*. A remarkable Difference between thefe and the *Kuriles* that inhabit the Iflands fituated farther towards the South, confiſts in this, that thofe wear long Hair; whereas thefe, have their Heads fhaved to the Neck; and when they falute any one, they bend their Knees. The foutherly *Kuriles* come fometimes hither for the fake of Trade; the Goods which they take back with them are, Sea Beavers, Foxes, and Eagles Feathers, wherewith they plume their Arrows.

Of the fame Nature is the fecond Ifland, *Purumufchur*, which is fituated only three or four Werfts from the firſt. The Inhabitants

make

make a Sort of Stuff, wove from Nettles, with which they cloath themselves; but they likewise get Silk and Cotton Stuffs, by trading with the remote *Kuriles*, and a Sort of Vessels, which probably must be Porcelaine. He praises their Valour and Dexterity in War: They use Bows and Arrows, and likewise Pikes and Sabres. They are, moreover, covered with Armour.

Passing a Streight with Baidares, lightly loaded, in sti.' Weather, in half a Day, there is the third Island, called *Muschu*, or *Onikutan*, which is also inhabited by *Kuriles*, who manufacture Stuffs made of Nettles, and catch Sea Beavers and Foxes. There are no Sables to be found in this and the two aforementioned Islands. The Inhabitants go, for the Sake of Hunting, to some Islands situated on its Side, and sometimes visit the Continent of *Kamtschatka*, where they buy Beavers, Foxes, and other Merchandize, and trade with these to the Islands situated farther to the South. Many of them understand the Language of the *Kamtschedales* situated on the River *Bolschaia*, with whom they trade and intermarry.

On the West Side of these three inhabited Islands, there are three uninhabited ones, in the following Order:

Ujachkupa, opposite the Island of *Schumtschi*, at some Distance: Upon it stands an high Mountain, which, in clear Weather, may be seen from the Mouth of the River *Bolschia*. The Inhabitants of the first and second Island, as likewise some from the Continent of *Kamtschatka*, come now and then over to this Island in the Hunting Season.

Sirinki, a small Island opposite the Streight, between the second and third Islands, towards the West.

Kukumiwa, likewise a small Island, situated to the South-west of the former. Both are visited by the Inhabitants of the before-mentioned Islands, in the Hunting Season.

We proceed in the Order of the Islands that extend themselves towards the South. The fourth is called *Araumakutan*, and is uninhabited: Upon it is a Volcano. The Streights between this Island and *Muschu*, as also that between this and the following Island *Siaskutan*, are but about half as broad as that between the second and third Islands.

Siaskutan, the fifth Island, has a few Inhabitants. This is the Market for the Inhabitants of the before-mentioned and following Islands, where they meet to trade.

Ikarma, is a small uninhabited Island, to the westward of *Siaskutan*.

Maschautsch is such another, South-west from *Ikarma*.

Igaitu, is an Island, like the former, to the South-east of *Siaskutan*. These three Islands are not reckoned in following the Order in which they extend to the South.

From

From *Siaskutan* it requires a whole Day to cross the Sea, with heavy laden Baidares, to the following Island *Schokoki*, which is to be considered as the sixth in Order. Between this and the following Island the Distance is but half as much.

Motogo, the seventh.
Schashowa, the eighth.
Uschischir, the ninth.
Kitui, the tenth Island.

These are all but small Islands, in which is nothing worthy of Observation, but that the Streights between them, and between *Kitui* and the following Island of *Schimuschir*, are so narrow, that one may row over, in light Baidares, in less than half a Day's Time; heavy laden Badaires require half a Day, and sometimes more. There is a strong Current between these Islands, especially at the Time of Ebb and Flood; which last rises very high in those Parts, and therefore many People lose their Lives in attempting to cross over at that Time. On the Island of *Kitui* there grow Reeds that are used for Arrows.

Schimuschir, the eleventh Island, is inhabited. From hence the Passage to the following Island, *Iturpu*, is something broader than the former.

Tschirpui, an Island out of the Number, is situated to the West of the Streights between *Schimuschir* and *Iturpu*. Upon it is an high Mountain.

Iturpu, the twelfth Island, is large, and well inhabited. The Inhabitants are called by the *Kuriles* of the aforementioned Islands, *Gych-Kuriles*. The *Japanese* call them *Eso*. Such *Kuriles* are also Possessors of the following Islands: Their Language and Manner of Living differ from the former; they shave their Heads; their Salutation consists in bending of the Knees; as to their Valour, and Dexterity in War, they may be preferred to the former. Great Forests, and various Sorts of wild Beasts, are found there, particularly Bears. Here and there are also Rivers, at the Mouths of which convenient Places are found wherein large Ships may anchor safe from the Winds and Waves: This has been particularly taken Notice of, because, on the other Islands, but little Wood is found, and no Convenience for large Ships.

After a small Passage we come to the thirteenth Island, named *Urup*, the Inhabitants of which are the same with those on *Iturpu*. They manufacture Stuffs spun from Nettles; but buy Cotton and Silk Stuffs at *Kunaschir*, and trade with them to the first and second Islands; from whence they bring back with them Sea Beavers, Foxes, and
Eagles

(xxxviii)

Eagles Feathers. It has been said for certain, that they are under no Subjection; which may be much more certainly concluded of the Inhabitants of *Iturpu*.

Between *Urup* is a narrow Streight, to the fourteenth Island *Kunafchir*, which is larger than either of those already mentioned. The Inhabitants are very numerous, and the same with the former; but whether they are a free People, or dependant on the Town of *Matmai*, on the Island of the same Name, is uncertain. As they frequently go over to *Matmai* on Account of Trade, so those of *Matmai* frequently come over to them. Many *Kamtschedales*, of both Sexes, are kept as Slaves upon *Iturpu*, *Urup*, *Kunaschir*, and *Matmai*. How far it is from *Kunaschir* to the Island of *Matmai*, is not certainly known.

The Island of *Matmai* is the 15th, and concludes this Range. It is the largest of all, and inhabited by the same People of *Eso*, or *Kytch-Kuriles*. The *Japanese* have built a Town on this Island, called by the same Name, *Matmai*, which stands upon the South West Shore, and is inhabited by *Japanese*. People are banished thither from *Japan*, and a Garrison kept there for the Defence of the Place, which is sufficiently provided with Cannon, Muskets, and all other Arms and warlike Stores. There are, besides, strong Guards on the East and West Coasts, to watch narrowly over every Thing that happens. The Inhabitants of the Island trade with those of the Town. Fish, Blubber, and Skins of Beasts, are the Merchandize carried to the Town.

Between the Island of *Matmai*, and the principal Island of the Empire of *Japan*, there is but a small Streight, over which the Navigation is not without Danger, on Account of the many rocky Capes on both Sides, particularly at the Time of Flood and Ebb.

Of *Japan* itself many Pieces of Intelligence were also received, of which I shall only mention the principal ones.

The Name of the chief Island is *Niphon*, after which the whole Empire is named. *Japan* is a Name entirely unknown on that Island; it is to be attributed to the *Portuguese*, who thus pronounce the *Chinese* Word, *Ge-puen*, properly, *Dschebyng*, whereby *Japan*, or rather *Niphon*, is called. The chief Town of the Country, in which the King *Kubosama* has his Residence, lies on the River *Jedo*, which empties itself into a great Bay, at a small Distance from the Town. The *Japanese* who told this, and many Things besides, at *Kamtschatka*, seemed to be worthy of Credit; since most of their Accounts agree with what we know of *Japan* from *Kaempfer* and others.

I cannot help observing one Thing, which contradicts the Discoveries made by the Ship *Castricom* in 1643, and all the Representations of

Jeso,

Jeso, which, since that Time, have been seen in Maps and Charts, viz. That, according to the Deposition of the *Kuriles* and *Japanese* at *Kamtschatka*, that Country is divided into several Islands; whereas, according to the former, they form only one great Island. We might, perhaps, have, here, Reason for Doubt, if every Thing mentioned by the *Japanese* was not confirmed by the Discoveries of our Navigators, as shall be shewn in its proper Place. It is probable, that the *Dutch* on board the Ship *Castricom* held the Streights between the Islands to be Bays; but what can be said to the swift Torrent observed in these Streights, at the Time of low and high Water? These ought not to have escaped the Observation of the *Dutch*; and if they did observe them, why did they not enquire into the Passages, and discover that, instead of one, there were several Islands? To reconcile these contradictory Accounts, a Medium may, perhaps, be found, that will prejudice neither Party. Suppose *Jeso* was, at the Time of the *Dutch* Navigation, really such a Country as is described by the People on board the Ship *Castricom*; but let us adopt, at the same Time, as a Thing well known, that our Earth is subject to many, and, frequently, strange Changes: Great Earthquakes swallow up Countries and Islands, and produce new ones. Now, Earthquakes are very usual in those Parts; therefore the Land of *Jeso* may, after the Voyage of the *Dutch*, have been torn into several lesser Islands by an Earthquake. This seems to be, at least, more equitable, than when Mess. *De Lisle* and *Buache* call in Question the modern Discoveries made in our Times, on Account of the Situation of the Land *Jeso* described by the Ship *Castricom*.

We shall make Mention of some other Islands, that are situated to the South of the River *Ud*, on the Continent of *Siberia*, and are commonly called the *Sebantarian* Islands. The Name seems to be old; for it has its Origin from the *Giljackes*, a People who dwell near the Mouth of the River *Amur*, and, about the Middle of the last Century, were subject to the *Russian* Empire, as I have shewn in *The History of the River Amur*. At that Time the *Russians*, probably, enquired of the *Giljackes* for the Name of this Island: These latter, not knowing any particular Name it had, answered, *Sebantar*, which signifies, in the *Giljackish* Language, an Island in general. Now, though from that Time these Islands were known to the *Russians*, yet we do not find, in written Accounts, that any Body had taken the Pains to make a more exact Enquiry about them, till, in the Year 1710, the Prince *Wasilei Iwanowitsch Gagarin*, among other Preparations at *Jakutzk*, committed this Affair to the Waywode *Trauernicht*. It was only known in general from the Relations of some *Cossacs* and *Tungusēs* who had been at *Udskoi Ostrog*,

Oſtrog, that theſe Iſlands may be ſeen from the Mouth of the River *Ud*; that the firſt Iſland is ſituated a Day's Voyage from the Continent; likewiſe the ſecond from the firſt, and the third from the ſecond, at the ſame Diſtance; that many Sables and Foxes are found upon them, and that the *Giljackes* uſed to viſit them merely on Account of Hunting; probably, becauſe the *Giljackes* have larger and ſtronger Veſſels than the *Tunguſes*, whoſe Canoes, of Birch Bark ſewed together, are not at all fit for croſſing the Sea. There were no written Accounts about it till after the Year 1709, when the Waywode *Trauernicht*, of his own Accord, ordered the Commander *Sorokoumow*, who was ſent to *Udſkoi Oſtrog*, to ſail to the *Schantarian* Iſlands, and make Enquiry in Relation to their Nature and Situation, bringing back to *Jakutzk* certain Intelligence of theſe Particulars: For although this was not done by him, yet he brought back with him written Depoſitions from the *Udſkoi Coſſacs* and *Tunguſes*, which contained the above Depoſitions.

Hereupon *Trauernicht* gave freſh Orders to the Commander *Waſilei Ignatiew* (who was ſent the following Year to *Udſkoi Oſtrog*) concerning the Navigation of the *Schantarian* Iſlands, and provided him, at the ſame Time, with every Neceſſary for building and equipping a Ship on the River *Ud*, in which the Navigation might be ſafely and conveniently made. The Commander of *Udſkoi* again charged ſome *Coſſacs* with this Commiſſion; who, in the Year 1712, ſet ſail with two Boats from *Udſkoi Oſtrog*, and followed the Coaſt as far as to the River *Tugur*. There they remained the whole Summer, to obtain a Supply of Fiſh, upon which they might live during their Voyage. In the mean while another Company of *Coſſacs* joined them, who had been diſpatched from *Udſkoi* for the ſame End. They together built a larger Veſſel, of the Sort uſed in the Frozen Sea; and having finiſhed it, they ſet ſail in *March* 1713. The Leader of this Company was called *Semoen Anabara*: They ſtill followed the Coaſt to a Promontory, from thence they rowed over the Sea, and in three Hours arrived at the firſt Iſland, on which they perceived neither Man or Beaſt, except one black Bear. Having paſſed the Night on this Iſland, they went to the ſecond, ſpending half a Day in the Paſſage: Here they alſo ſaw nothing but Bears; wherefore, on the third Day, they paſſed to the third Iſland; how long they were on their Paſſage is not mentioned. They arrived there on the 29th of *June*, and finding Sables and Foxes, they had the Hopes of obtaining great Advantages by Hunting, and therefore reſolved to ſtay there the following Winter. They found a Woman, whoſe Language they did not underſtand (probably a *Giljack* Woman); having kept her a Month with them, ſhe was loſt, without their knowing

what

what became of her. *Anabara* sent some of his People to the River *Tugur*, to fetch a fresh Supply of Fish, but they did not come back; only four remained with him on the Island, and the Want of Provisions hindered any Intelligence being got of its Extent, and other Properties; for no one went above a Day's Journey from their Place of Abode; this the Hunting of Sables required, since, on every Side, at that Distance, Traps were set, which every Day were looked after, to see if any Sables were caught in them: There were also Wolves and Bears on the Island. The Woods consist of Larch Trees, Firs, Birch, and Aspens. Two of the Company died on the Island, and three sailed back to the Continent on the 29th of *June*, 1714, where they arrived on the first of *July* following, without landing on any other of the Islands. From thence they came, in ten Days, to the River *Ud*, when they arrived at *Udskoi Ostrog*. After their Arrival at *Jakutzk*, an Account of their Voyage was taken down in Writing in the Chancery, on the 20th of *October* in the same Year, which is the Materials from whence I have compiled this Relation.

Hitherto there was no other Way to *Kamtschatka*, but by *Anadirsk*, which was attended with great Fatigue and Expence, and was very Dangerous on Account of the *Korjacks*, who commonly lay in Wait for the *Russians*, that travelled either to or from *Kamtschatka*, killed them and divided the Booty among themselves. This occasioned the Proposal of seeking a Way to it by Sea from *Ochotzk*.

Indeed they wanted at *Ochotzk*, Vessels fit to navigate the Sea; nor was the Use of Compass known there, till, in the Year 1714, by express Orders from the great Emperor *Peter* I. the Governor Prince *Gagarin* supplied this two-fold Deficiency. In the Beginning the Governor might think they would be able to do without the Assistance of these, for his first Order relating to the Navigation by Sea to *Kamtschatka* dated *Feb.* 17, 1713, and directed to the Waywode *Jeltschin*, contains nothing about Ship-building, or People experienced in Navigation. But then the Consequence of this too was nothing else than the Arrival of the *Dworanin Iwan Sorokaumow*, at *Ochotzk*, who was charged with the Affair at *Jakutzk*, and came in the Autumn of the same Year with twelve *Cossacs*; but after having committed many Disorders there, he was brought back under an Arrest to *Jakutzk*, without having done any thing worthy of Notice. It was highly necessary therefore, for the Governor to send thither immediately some Sailors and Ship-carpenters. These arrived at *Jakutzk* on the 23d of *May* 1714, under the Conduct of a *Cossac*, named *Cosmas Sokolow*, with twenty other *Cossacs*; and were

were difpatched to *Ochotzk* on the third of *July*; and by thefe the Difcovery was made.

One of the Sailors who was a *Dutchman*, a Native of *Hoorn*, named *Henry Bufh*, was ftill alive at *Jakutzk* in 1736, when I refided there, and upon my Enquiry, told me the following particulars.

After their Arrival at *Ochotzk*, the Carpenters built a Veffel for the Sea Service, after the Manner of the *Ruffian* Loddies, with which they formerly ufed to fail from *Archangel* to *Mefen*, *Puftofero*, and *Nova Zembla*. This Work took them up the Year 1715. The Veffel was a very good and durable one. It was eight Fathoms and a half long, three Fathoms broad; and drew, when laden, three Feet and a half of Water. The firft Voyage was undertaken in *June* 1716. They followed the North-eaft Coaft, as far as the Country about the River *Ola*, and wanted to continue this Courfe ftill farther; but a contrary Wind drove the Veffel acrofs the Sea to *Kamtfchatka*. It was a Promontory which they firft got fight of, fituated North of the Mouth of the River *Tigil*, where they caft Anchor. Some of the Company went afhore to feek Men; but found only empty Huts. The *Kamtfchedales* had obferved the Approach of the Veffel, and out of Fear were fled into the Woods and Mountains. Hereupon our Navigators fet Sail again, paffed the *Tigil*, and arrived in one Day at the Brook *Charinfowka*, near which two fmall Iflands are fituated. The firft, which is the largeft, lies about five Werfts from the Continent. The fecond, confifting merely of Rocks, is a little farther. From *Charinfowka* they arrived the following Day at the River *Itfcha*, having kept the Sea all Night, and failed to the Land in the Morning: Here they put fome People afhore; but found neither Men nor Habitations, and foon came back: Wherefore they followed the Coaft ftill farther, and came to the River *Krutogorowa*. They intended to make this River, but miffed its Mouth; and finding a convenient Bay to the South of the River, they caft Anchor. In fearching the Country, they met with a *Kamtfchedale* Girl, who was feeking in the Fields for Roots fit for eating, and fhe fhewed them *Kamtfchedale* Habitations, in which then dwelt twelve *Kamtfchedale Coffacs*, who were there in order to receive the Tribute; and they being fent for, ferved for Guides and Interpreters. The Veffel was brought to the Mouth of the River *Kompakowa*, and it was refolved to winter there. At that Time the Sea caft upon the Shore a Whale that had in its Body an Harpoon of *European* Workmanfhip, marked with *Roman* Letters. In the Beginning of the Month of *May*, 1717, they put to Sea again; but it was yet full of Ice. On the fourth Day after their Departure they happened to be ftuck faft between the Ice, and were

obliged

obliged to continue in this Manner five Weeks and three Days, before they could proceed on their Voyage; at last they regained the Coast of *Ochotzk*, between the River *Ola* and *Tauiskoi Ostrog*; where they staid several Days, and returned, about the Middle of *July*, to *Ochotzk*. From this Time there has been a continual Navigation between *Ochotzk* and *Kamtschatka*.

In 1718, the *Sin-bojarkoi Procofei Philkeew*, was sent on the Discovery of the *Schantarian* Islands. This Man was yet alive when I was at *Jakutzk*; he informed me that their Number is not determined; that the largest is about twenty Werfts long from North to South, and from three to four Werfts broad, and that it is to be seen from the Mouth of the River *Ud*.

In the Beginning of 1719, the Czar sent two Navigators, *Iwan Jevreinow* and *Fedor Luschin*, to *Kamtschatka*, with Instructions in his own Hand Writing, and an Order to all the *Siberian* Commanders, that in all things they should be assisted, if they desired it. They arrived at *Jakutzk* in *May*, 1720, went over to *Kamtschatka* the same Summer, and returned to *Jakutzk* in 1721, but kept their Transactions secret; therefore we cannot know what they did, while we have no Opportunity of consulting their Instructions. In the mean while, if we may judge from the Consequences, the Aim of their Expedition was limited merely to the *Kurilian* Islands; and perhaps chiefly to that, from whence, according to Report, the *Japanese* fetched Ore. *Henry Bush*, the *Dutch* Sailor, conducted them. The first Summer he brought them from *Ochotzk* to *Bolscheretzkoi Ostrog*; and the following Year they sailed by the *Kurilian* Islands. On coming to the fifth of them (which may be the sixth, as *Bush* may have made a Mistake in the Number) they came to an Anchor: *Bush* advised them to the contrary, as the Ground was rocky; but was obliged to obey. They lost four Anchors while there, which were all they had, for the Cables were torn to pieces by the Stones and Rocks; but thro' great good Fortune they returned to *Kamtschatka* without farther Damage. Here they made Wooden Anchors, to which they fastened great Stones, and thus sailed the next Summer to *Ochotzk*. This I have from the Mouth of the Sailor. *Jevreinow* left *Luschin*, his Companion, behind him in *Siberia*, and went to the Czar with on Account of his Voyage, and a Map of the *Kurilian* Islands, as far as he had discovered them, in the Month of *May*, 1722.

VOYAGES

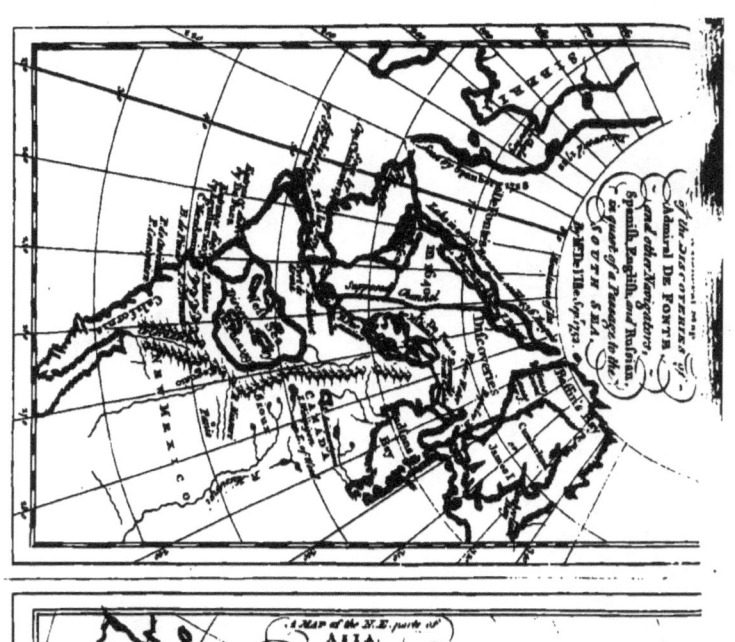
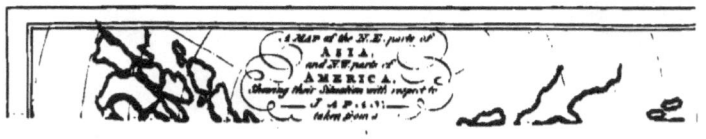

VOYAGES

FROM

ASIA to *AMERICA*.

THE Czar, *Peter the Great*, being curious to know whether *Asia* and *America* were contiguous, or seperated by a wide or narrow channel of the sea, wrote the following instructions with his own hand, and ordered the chief Admiral Count *Fedor Matfewitsch Apraxin*, to see them carried into execution.

I. *One or two Boats with decks to be built at* Kamtschatka, *or at any other convenient place, with which*

II. *Enquiry should be made in relation to the northerly coasts, to see whether they were not contiguous with* America, *since their end was not known. And this done, they should*

III. *See whether they could not somewhere find an harbour belonging to* Europeans, *or an European ship. They should likewise set apart some men, who were to enquire after the name and situation of the coasts discovered. Of all this an exact journal should be kept, with which they should return to* Petersburg.

The Empress *Catharine*, as she endeavoured in all points to execute most precisely the plans of her deceased husband, in a manner began her reign with an order for the expedition to *Kamtschatka*.

Vitus Bering, at that time Captain of a ship, was nominated commander of this expedition, and two Lieutenants, *Martin Spangberg*, and *Alexei Tschirikow*, were his assistants, together with other sea officers of inferior rank; they also had some along with them that

B

understood

VOYAGES

FROM

ASIA to *AMERICA*.

THE Czar, *Peter the Great*, being curious to know whether *Asia* and *America* were contiguous, or seperated by a wide or narrow channel of the sea, wrote the following instructions with his own hand, and ordered the chief Admiral Count *Fedor Matfewitsch Apraxin*, to see them carried into execution.

I. One or two Boats with decks to be built at Kamtschatka, or at any other convenient place, with which

II. *Enquiry should be made in relation to the northerly coasts, to see whether they were not contiguous with* America, *since their end was not known. And this done, they should*

III. *See whether they could not somewhere find an harbour belonging to* Europeans, *or an* European *ship. They should likewise set apart some men, who were to enquire after the name and situation of the coasts discovered. Of all this an exact journal should be kept, with which they should return to* Petersburg.

The Empress *Catharine*, as she endeavoured in all points to execute most precisely the plans of her deceased husband, in a manner began her reign with an order for the expedition to *Kamtschatka*.

Vitus Bering, at that time Captain of a ship, was nominated commander of this expedition, and two Lieutenants, *Martin Spangberg*, and *Alexei Tschirikow*, were his assistants, together with other sea officers of inferior rank; they also had some along with them that understood ship building. The day of their departure from *Petersburg* was the 5th of *February*, 1725. On the 16th of *March* they reached *Tobolsk*, the chief town of *Siberia*, where they remained till the 16th of *May*, as well to wait for the convenience of a passage by water, as to take with them several mechanicks and materials, which they wanted for their voyage. The following summer was spent in navigating the rivers *Irtsch*, *Ob*, *Ret*, *Jenisei*, *Tunguska* and *Ilim*, after which they found themselves under the necessity of wintering in the *Ilimsk*, and, in the mean while, took in provisions for a longer voyage.

In the spring of 1726, they sailed down the river *Lena* to *Jakutzk*; Lieut. *Spangberg* went immediately before them upon the rivers *Aldan*, *Maia*, and *Judoma*, with part of the provisions, and heavy naval stores. He was followed by Capt. *Bering* by land, with another part of the provisions that were packed upon horses; while Lieut. *Tschirikow* staid at *Jakutzk*, in order to bring by land the rest of the provisions. This division was necessary, on account of the toilsome way between *Jakutzk* and *Ochotzk*, it being not passable in summer with waggons, or in winter with sledges, on account of the marshes and rocky ground, and the country's not being at all inhabited, except in the neighbourhood of *Jakutzk*.

Lieut. *Spangberg*'s voyage was as unfortunate as Capt. *Bering*'s was successful, since he did not reach *Judomskoi Krest*, the place to which he was bound, but was frozen up in the river *Judoma*, at the mouth of the little river *Gorbei*. He set out on the 4th of *November* to go a foot to *Judomskoi Krest*, and *Ochotzk*, with the most necessary naval stores, but suffered so much with hunger by the way, that he was obliged to support life by eating leather bags, straps, and shoes; at length he arrived at *Ochotzk*, on the 1st of *January*, 1727. In the begining of *February* he returned to the *Judoma* to fetch the rest of his lading; but, as this was not sufficient, a third party, who were dispatched with horses from *Ochotzk*, assisted in transporting every thing happily. Upon this, on the 30th of *July*, Lieut. *Tschirikow*, with the last provisions, arrived also from *Jakutzk*.

In the mean while a vessel had been built at *Ochotzk*, named the *Fortuna*, which set sail on the 30th of *June*, under the command of Lieut. *Spangberg*, to transport to *Bolscheretzkoi* the most necessary naval stores, and some ship carpenters. This ship returned, together with the old vessel, which still remained, ever since the year 1716, when the navigation between *Ochotzk* and *Kamtschatka* began.

On

On the 21st of *August*, Capt. *Bering*, and Lieut. *Tschirikow*, began their voyage; they entered the mouth of the river *Bolschia*, on the 2d of *September*, and went the following winter, together with Lieut. *Spangberg*, from *Bolscheretzkoi* to *Nischnei Kamschatkoi Ostrog*, whither the ship carpenters went before them, in the summer, to fell wood for building of ships; they carried along with them as much provisions, and naval stores, as they believed were necessary, with which they went on very slowly, on account of the tedious carriage with dogs. On the 4th of *April* 1728, a boat was put upon the stocks, like the packet boats used in the *Baltick*; and, on the 10th of *July*, was launched, and named the boat *Gabriel*. This being provided with all necessary stores and provisions for forty men, during a year's voyage, they did not delay accomplishing the chief point they had in view.

For this end, Capt. *Bering* went to sea, from the mouth of the river *Kamtschatka*, on the 20th of *July*, of the abovementioned year, and steered North East, generally in sight of the coast of *Kamtschatka*; his chief endeavour was to describe this coast as exactly as possible upon a map, in which he succeeded pretty well, at least we have none better than this. On the 8th of *August*, being in the latitude of 64d. 30m. eight men of the *Tschuktschi* came rowing from the shore in a leathern canoe, called a *baidare*, formed of seal-skins, in order to inform themselves about the intention of this voyage. These people were conversed with by means of a *Rorjak* interpreter, and invited aboard the ship, upon which one of them, by means of two blown up seal-skins tied to a pole, came swimming to the ship, and was followed by all in the canoe. The captain obtained information from them, of the situation of the coast, and learnt that they would find it turn'd towards the West. Whether they made any enquiry about the opposite islands, or coasts, or not, is not mentioned in the captain's account, of which this is an extract. One may almost believe they were not thought of, since our navigators had no knowledge at all of what had been done before them, and consequently could not suppose the land so near. They heard of an island, which was said to lie somewhat farther, at no great distance from the continent; to this they gave the name of *St Lawrence*, on account of its being the 10th of *August*, that saint's day, when they pass'd by it, without observing any thing upon it, besides cottages of fishermen.

At last they arrived, on the 15th of *August*, in 67 deg. 18 min. North latitude, at a promontory, behind which the coast extended towards the West, as the former *Tschuktschi* had said. From this the captain drew a pretty plausible conclusion, that now he had reached the extremity of *Asia* towards the North East. He was of opinion that from thence the coast must continually run to the West; and was this the case, no connection with *America* could take place; consequently he believed that he had fulfilled his orders, and therefore proposed to the officers and the rest of the ships company, " That it " was time to think of their return. If they should sail further to " the North, it was to be feared they might meet with ice, in which " they might be involved, so as not easily to extricate themselves; " the usual thick fogs, in autumn, which already began to appear, " might rob them of a free prospect; and, in case a contrary wind " should arise, it would be almost impossible for them to return to " *Kamtschatka* that summer, and yet it was not adviseable to winter in " those parts, since the well known want of wood in all the northerly " regions towards the frozen sea, the savages of the country not yet " reduced to the obedience of the *Russian* government, and the steep " rocks, every where found along the shore, between which there was " not anchorage nor harbour, rendered it too dangerous."

It must be allowed that the circumstances, on which the captain founded his judgment, was false; for it was afterwards found that this was the promontory which, by the inhabitants of *Anadirskoi Ostrog*, is called *Serdze Kamen*, on account of a rock upon it in the form of a heart. And, although the country behind it winds to the West, yet this winding composes only a large bay, in the innermost part of which the rock *Matkol* lies, according to the above account given by the Cossack *Popow*. But here the coast begins again to run regularly to the North and North East, till in the 70th degree or more, of North latitude, the proper *Tschuktschian Noss*, as a great peninsula, appears; where, and not before, it might be said, that there was no connection between the two parts of the world, but who on board that ship could know this? For the particular and true knowledge of the country of the *Tschuktschi* is owing to my geographical researches made at *Jakutzk*, in the years 1736, and 1737. It may suffice, that in the chief point there was no mistake, and that *Asia* is really separated from *America* by a channel which connects the frozen sea with the *Pacific* Ocean.

They

(5)

They returned without any thing remarkable happening; but only, on the 20th of *August*, 40 men of the *Tschuktschi* came rowing to the ship in four Baidares, and brought presents, consisting of the flesh of rain-deer, fish, fresh-water, fox-skins, white foxes, and sea-horse teeth; for which they were rewarded with needles, steels for striking fire, iron, &c. On the 29th they came to an anchor on the coast of *Kamtschatka* in foggy and stormy weather; and, as the following morning the cable was torn to pieces in attempting to weigh the anchor, they were obliged to leave it behind them. On the 20th of *September* they returned to the river *Kamtschatka*, went up it, and took again their winter quarters at *Nischnei Kamtschatskoi Ostrog*.

Our sea officers frequently heard relations of the inhabitants of *Kamtschatka*, that were important enough to merit their observation, since, according to them, a country must be at no great distance towards the East, the discovery of which, and following its coasts afterwards was their duty; they themselves had not observed such great and high waves, as, in other places, are common in the open sea; they had seen fir-trees swimming in the sea, tho' they do not grow in *Kamtschatka*. Some even assured them, that they had seen this nearly situated land, in clear weather, from the elevated coasts of *Kamtschatka*.

Now the captain, willing to be assured of the truth, made preparations for another voyage, and disposed things in such a manner, that the return might not be by the way of *Kamtschatka*, but immediately to *Ochotzk*; and, on the 5th of *June* 1729, he set sail the second time, but a violent wind did not suffer him to leave the coasts at a greater distance than about 200 Wersts; and, meeting in the mean while with no land, he sailed back, and steered round the South promontary of *Kamtschatka**, the proper situation and form of which he described in his map, and returned by sea to the mouth of the river *Belschaia*, whence he went to *Ochotzk* on the 23d of *July*.

Hence he travelled on the 29th of the same month to *Judomskoi Krest*, there he found some small vessels, built floats, and with them went down the rivers *Judoma*, *Maia*, and *Aldan*. At *Belskoi Perewoss*, which is a passage over the *Aldan*, at the river *Bela*, he again took horses of the neighbouring *Jakutes*; with these he arrived, on the 29th of *August*, at *Jakutzk*, and set out from thence on the 10th of

* This is called by some *Cape Oskoi*, perhaps *Oskoi* has its origin from the *Russian* word for Southerly.

September,

September, in order to proceed by water up the *Lena* as far as possible The violent driving of the ice obliged him to stop on the 10th of *October*, at *Peleduiskaia Stoboda*, but this lasted no longer than till the 29th of the same month, when he proceeded on his travels with sledges. He took his way by *Ilimsk, Jeniseisk, Tomsk*, and *Tara*, to *Tobolsk*, where he staid from the 10th to the 25th of *January*, and returned on the 1st of *March* 1730, to *Petersburg*.

A little before a mistake had slipt into the geography of foreign countries, as if *Kamtschatka* was the same with the land of *Jeso*, and consequently extended towards the South, as far as the neighbourhood of *Japan*.

Two maps published soon after the death of *Peter the Great* (*a*) had occasioned this. They were confided in, as founded on the newest discoveries, and the affair was confirmed in the remarks of the *Swedish* officers, who had been prisoners in *Siberia*, annexed to the history of *Tartary*, written by *Abulgasi Bayadur Chan* (*b*). Therefore this hypothesis was also adopted by *Scheuchzer*, on his publishing *Kaempfer*'s history of *Japan* (*c*). M. *Strahlenberg* seemed to give it new weight by his testimony (*d*). M. *de Martiniere* (*e*) followed him with his applause, as well as M. *Bellin* (*f*), who added another new mistake, as if from the mouth of the river *Lena* to *Kamtschatka*, there was a common navigation, by means of which a trade was carried on to this country. Tho' this was not so much owing to M. *Bellin*, as to the author of the remarks to *Abulgasi*, he having first mentioned it (*g*).

Mr *Bering*, who had sailed about the South point of *Kamtschatka*, in the 51st degree of North latitude, rectifies their mistakes, and his map was sent to *Paris*, and incorporated with *Du Halde*'s, or rather

(*a*) A new map of the whole empire of *Great Russia*, in the condition in which it was found on the death of *Peter the Great*, and *Asiatic Russia*, drawn from the map published by order of the late Czar. There is also a map by *Homan*, engraved according to these.
(*b*) A genealogical history of the *Tartars*, pag. 109.
(*c*) History of *Japan* by M. *Kaempfer*, Vol. I. Preliminary discourses, page 17, and the eighth plate belonging to it.
(*d*) The north and east parts of *Europe* and *Asia*, Introduction, page 31, and the map belonging to it.
(*e*) Geographical dictionary, Vol. V. under the word *Kamtschatka*.
(*f*) History of *Japan* by Father *Charlevoix*, Vol. II. page 493, and the map to which he refers.
(*g*) L. c. page 108.

D'An-

D'Anville's Atlafs. Father *Caftel* (*h*) hence took an opportunity to refute M. *Bellin*, and the latter defended the miftake (*i*), thinking *Bering*'s map, in *Du Halde*'s Atlafs, had been a fufficient authority, and that M. *D'Anville* had been miftaken. But nothing is more certain than that this map had Capt. *Bering* himfelf for its author. M. *Swan Kirilow*, the chief fecretary of the directing fenate, and afterwards counfellor of ftate, had inferted the moft effential part of it, in his general map of *Ruffia*, before *Du Halde*'s work was publifhed; for his map was already finifhed in 1732, and publifhed in 1734, therefore M. *D'Anville* could not be miftaken. M. *Bellin* fhould have read what Father *Du Halde* (*k*) himfelf fays of the means by which he came by this map, and it would have eafily convinced him of the contrary.

While Capt. *Bering* made the laft voyage from the river *Kamtfchatka* towards the Eaft, a *Japannefe* veffel was again driven to the coaft of *Kamtfchatka*, where it ftranded in *July* 1729, South of the bay of *Awatfcha*. A chief of 50 *Coffacks*, named *Andreas Schtinnikow*, came hither with fome *Kamtfchedales*, when the *Japannefe* had juft brought their goods afhore from the fhip. *Schtinnikow* received fome prefents from them, but this did not fatisfy him; for, after fpending two days among the *Japannefe*, he left them in the night time, and concealed himfelf with his company in the neighbournood, in order to fee how they would proceed. The *Japannefe* afflicted at *Schtinnikow*'s departure, wanted to feek for other inhabitants, for which purpofe they took a boat, and fteered along the coaft; upon which *Schtinnikow* ordered the *Kamtfchedales* to follow them, and to fhoot them all except two, which they did, fo that out of 17 *Japannefe* there remained alive only an old man, and a boy of 11 years old. *Schtinnikow*, having taken poffeffion of all their effects, and caufed their fhip to be broke to pieces, in order to make ufe of the iron, he took the two *Japannefe* as prifoners of war, or rather as flaves to *Werchnei Kamtfchatfkoi Oftrog*. This barbarity fhewn to fhipwreck'd ftrangers could not remain unpunifhed. *Schtinnikow* having taken his tryal, received the halter for his reward, but the *Japannefe* were fent to *Jakutzk* in 1731, and from thence to *Tobolfk*, after which, in 1732, they were brought to *Peterfburg*.

(*h*) Differtation on the celebrated land of *Kamtfchatka*, in the Memoirs of *Trevoux* for *July* 1737, pag. 1156, and following.
(*i*) Memoirs of *Trevoux* for *Auguft* 1737, page 2389, and following.
(*k*) Defcription of *China*, Vol. IV. page 561.

Here

(8)

Here they were for some time instructed in the *Russian* language, and the principles of the christian religion, and became christians. The first was baptized by the name of *Cusmas*, and the second by that of *Damian*, for they were before called *Sosa* and *Gonsa*. Hereupon they were sent, by order of the directing senate, to the academy of sciences. They brought up scholars who were able to read and write tolerable good *Japannese*, when, in the years 1736 and 1739, their masters died. They called the the town of their nativity *Satzma*. *Kaempfer* writes this name *Satzuma* On the maps, according to the *Portuguese* pronunication, it is called *Saxuma*. It is a town and province on the South West of the island of *Ximo*, otherwise called *Kiusiu*. *Sosa* had been a merchant; the father of *Gonsa* had been a pilot on board the *Japannese* fleet, and the son chose the same way of life. Their vessel which they called *Wakaschimar*, was freighted with cotten and silk stuffs, rice, and paper. As they were destined for *Osacka*, the commander of the town of *Satzma*, named *Inatzdare Osina Nokam*, had given them the rice and paper, the first of which was to serve for the food of the inhabitants, no rice growing at *Osacka*, and the second was for the use of the public offices, but they never got to *Osacka*, having been distressed by storms, and driven about on the sea for six months, till at last they were stranded on *Kamtschatka*, on the 8th of *July*. The capital of the empire they called *Kio*; it is situated on the river *Jedogaw*, which is there about a werst broad, and at a small distance from the town falls into the sea. The king of *Japan* they called *Osma*, and gave more accounts of the same nature, but the inserting them here would not be to our purpose.

The chief of the *Jakutzk Cossacks* named, *Asanassei Scheftakows*, presented several proposals to the senate to render the obstinate *Tschuktschi* tributary, as also the *Korjaks*, who inhabited as well the *Siberian* coast of the *Penschinskanian* gulf, as both coasts of the North parts of *Kamtschatka*, and had often revolted. He was desirous of discovering the country opposite *Tschukztskoi Nofs*, and of summoning its inhabitants to the obedience of *Russia*. He resolved to make another attempt to discover the pretended country in the frozen sea, and finally he comprised also the *Schantarian* and *Kurilian* islands in the enquiries he was to make. The eloquence with which he brought his proposals on the carpet, and laid them before persons of all ranks, and the benefit that might be derived from them, procured him a great deal of applause. He was appointed the chief of a particular

expe-

expedition, in which he was to accomplish all he had promised. The admiralty office at *Petersburg* appointed one *Jacob Hens* for his Pilot; *Iwan Fedorow* for his second mate; *Michael Gwosdew* for his geodesist, or navigator; *Herdebol* for a searcher of ore, and ten sailors. He was provided at *Catherineburg* * with small cannon and mortars, with all their appurtenances. At *Tobolsk*, a captain of the *Siberian* regiment of dragoons, named *Dmitri Pawluzki*, was ordered to join him, and they both had the command of 400 *Cossacks*, having moreover all the *Cossacks* at their command who were garrison'd in the *Ostroges* and *Simowies* within the *Tschukutsch* jurisdiction, to which they should come.

With these dispatches *Scheslakow* returned from *Petersburg* to *Siberia*, in the month of *June* 1727. At *Tobolsk* he tarried till the 28th of *November*, spent the winter in the upper huts of the *Lena*, and arrived at *Jakutzk* in the summer 1728. Here a great dispute arose between *Scheslakow* and *Pawlutzki*, which probably occasioned their separation, though both had the same design in their intended enterprises. *Scheslakow* went in 1729 to *Ochotzk*, and there for his use took possession of the vessels with which captain *Bering* was lately come back from *Kamtschatka*. Having dispatched on the first of *September* his cousin *Sinbojarski Iwan Scheslakow*, in the boat *Gabriel*, to the river *Ud*, from whence he was to proceed to *Kamtschatka*,

* *Catherineburg*. A new city, begun in the year 1721, in the government of *Siberia*, in the province of *Ugor*, on the river *Isett*, between the *Uralian* mountains, and had this name given it, in honour to the late Empress *Catharine*. This place is five hundred and fifty *Wersts* from the city of *Tobolski*. The fortification is square, and has six whole, and four half bastions: The river *Isett* runs through it, along which is a great dam made, and near it the following works and manufactures are set on foot: (1) Two high mast-ovens: (2) Four mills with hammers for drawing iron bars: (3) Three mills with hammers for flatting plate iron: (4) Two fabricks, for making of plates for tin, with a stone building where the plates are tinn'd: (5) A fabrick for working rough steel, containing two small hammer works, and eight forges: (6) A steel fabrick with two hammer works: (7) A wire fabrick: (8) Two machines for making iron hoops: (9) A machine for cutting iron into small bars for course wire and nails: (10) A mill for hammering of anchors: (11) Two machines for making sword-blades: (12) A machine for boring and polishing cannon: (13) Six furnaces to melt copper: (14) A saw-mill with three frames; all these works are kept going by forty-two water wheels. The directors of these several works, are mostly *Germans*, each of whom has a house to himself, all built in a regular and uniform manner; they have, besides the *Russian*, a church of their own, and a *German* minister, who also teaches their children reading, writing, and the languages.

C
and

and enquire into and describe the islands lying within this navigation; he himself went with the other vessel, called the *Fortuna*, to *Tauiskoi Ostrog*, but had the misfortune to suffer shipwreck on his way, and to see the greatest part of the men he had with him perish in the water, narrowly escaping himself alive with four others in a canoe. On the 30th of *September* he sent from *Tauiskow Ostrog*, *Iwan Ostasiew*, a *Cossack*, with some *Korjack* elders, before him along the coast, with orders to go to the river *Penschina*, and to persuade, by fair promises to obedience the obstinate *Korjaks* dwelling in the places he should go through. He himself followed in the beginning of *December* with the rest of his people, overtook *Ostasiew* on the road, and arrived fortunately within two days journey from the river *Penschina*, where he met an innumerable swarm of *Tschuktschi*, who were on their march to make war against the *Korjak's* elders. So inconsiderable were *Scheslakow's* company of *Russians*, added to the *Ochozsk Tunguses* †, *Lamutes*, and *Korjaks* he had

† *Tunguß*. This is a most numerous and most straggling Pagan nation (with respect to their dwellings) that is in *Siberia*, and are supposed to amount to 70 or 80000 men. These people are, in general, distinguished by three names, viz. *Konni Tunguß*, *Oleni Tunguß*, and *Sabatschi Tunguß*, that is, those that make use of horses for riding and draught, those who use rein-deer for that purpose, and those who use dogs. In the same manner as the *Finlandians* have been distinguished formerly, by some writers, into *Skrete* and *Rede*; i. e. into skaiting *Finlandians*, and such as used sledges. The *Russians* in *Siberia* give, besides, to the latter sort of these *Tunguß*, divers other names, as *Podkumena*, *Tumaki*, and *Wonki Tunguß*, &c. because the latter have very disagreeable smells, occasioned by the fish, and other uncommon things they feed upon; and the former live in and about the mountains: In other things they are no way different from the *Sabatschi Tunguß*. The *Jakubti* call them *Udschtnen*, from the word *Ud*, signifying a *Dog*: Whence also a Capital river, which discharges itself into the bay of *Lama*, on account of these people, who keep dogs, that have hair one fourth of an ell long, is named *Ud-Reka*, i. e. the *river of dogs*. Moreover, these *Sabatschi Tunguß* living partly at the point of the bay of *Penschin* or *Lama*, and partly near the rivers *Aldan*, *Tungur*, and *Ud*, the *Russians* have given that point the name of *Sabatschi Nos*. The *Sabatschi Tunguß* are subdivided among themselves into divers tribes, viz. 1. *Lamunka*. 2. *Kæltaku*, which is the largest and strongest. 3. *Lakigir*. 4. *Brangathal*. 5. *Ninengath*. 6. *Bugagi*. 7. *Maimogur*. 8. *Boldati*. 9. *Sologon*. 10. *Mamour*. 11. *Ilogin*. 12. *Kotnochan*; and, 13. *Jukagri* or *Jukairi*. As to the two other sorts, viz. the *Kouni* and *Oeeni Tunguß*, they are sufficiently described in the travels of *Isbrand Idet*, and in those of *Adam Brant*, where it is observable, that both these writers are of opinion, the *Konni-Tunguß*, as well as the *Targuzini*, came originally from *Dauria*, and that the *Oleni-Tunguß*, who live near the river *Angara*, are all one people with the *Konni*, tho' their tongues are different; and the account of the above authors, with my table, taken together, will pretty well clear up what I have said concerning this nation. That their ancestors were those primitive *Tartars*, who are called in ancient *European* authors, by the name of *Abii*.

with

with him, that they amounted in all to no more than 150 men; this did not prevent him from venturing an engagement with the *Tfchuktfchi*. It, however, had an unfortunate issue, *Scheftakow* was shot by an arrow from the enemy, and he fell to the ground, and those of his men who escaped with their lives, were dispersed. This happened on the 14th of *March* 1730, near the brook of *Jegatfch*, which, between the rivers *Paren* and *Penfchina*, falls in the *Penfchinfkin* gulph.

Three days before this unhappy accident, *Scheftakow* sent orders to *Tauifkoi Oftrog*, that the *Coffack*, *Tryphon Krupifchew*, should go to *Bolfcheretzkoi Oftrog*, in a veffel adapted for the sea, from thence double the southern headland of *Kamtfchatka*, make the harbour of *Nifchnei Kamtfchatzkoi Oftrog*, and proceed farther with the fame veffel to the river *Anadir*, and invite the inhabitants of the large country opposite to it, to pay tribute to *Ruffia*. If *Gwofdew*, the navigator, chose to go in this expedition, he should take him on board the veffel, and shew him respect. There are no intelligences of what were the consequences of these orders; we only know that, in the year 1730, *Gwofdew*, the navigator, was actually between 65 and 66 degrees of north latitude, on a strange coast situate opposite, at a small distance from the country of the *Tfchuktfchi*, and that he found people there, but could not speak with them, for want of an interpreter.

In the mean while, the *Sinbojarfkoi Iwan Scheftakow* was sailed to *Kamtfchatka* in the boat *Gabriel*, and arrived at *Bolfcheretzkoi* the 19th of *September*. For, though he had been enjoined first to go to the river *Ud*, yet that he could not compleat, on account of a strong contrary wind. The following summer he made the voyage to the river *Ud*, and arrived at *Udfkoi Oftrog*, where he found people, who had been sent thither by the chief *Scheftakow*, and had built a very indifferent veffel; he sailed back to *Kamtfchatka*, and both going and coming back saw several islands, and at last returned to *Ochotzk*. I regret that I am not able to mention the particular circumstances of this voyage, as no journal was kept at sea. However, in an account, which, on, the 23d of *October* 1730, was delivered to the *Jakutzk* company by the *Sinbojarfkoi Iwan Scheftakow*, the days are noted on which every thing was done; these we will add as a proof.

June 16, 1730, departure from *Bolschaia reka*.
July 16. ——— arrival at the river *Ud*.
. 19, ——— arrival at *Udskoi Ostrog*.
. 28, ——— departure from thence.
Aug. 13, ——— arrival at *Bolschaia reka*.
. 20, ——— departure from thence.
Sept. 5, ——— arrival at *Ochotzk*.

Just at a time when *Scheftakow* came back to *Ochotzk*, *Jacob Hens*, the pilot, received an order from captain *Pawlutzki*, who in the mean while had advanced from *Jakutzk* by the usual land road to *Nischnee Kolymskoe Simowie*, or *Ostrog*, that, although advice had been received by the way of *Anadirskoi Ostrog*, of the death of *Scheftakow*, chief of the *Cossacks*, yet it would occasion no impediment to the expedition; that the pilot *Hens* should, with one of the vessels left at *Ochotzk* by captain *Bering*, come round *Kamtschatka* to *Anadirsk*, for which place he, captain *Pawlutzki*, would shortly depart, &c.

In consequence of this order, *Hens* took the boat *Gabriel*, and sailed to *Kamtschatka*. The 20th of *July* 1731, he was at the mouth of the river *Kamtschatka*, in order to proceed on his voyage to the river *Anadir*, when he received intelligence, that on the same day a rebellious band of *Kamtschedales* were come to *Nischnei Kamtschatzkoi Ostrog*, had killed most of the *Russians* there, and set fire to the houses of the inhabitants. The remaining few *Russians* took shelter in the vessel, and *Hens* sent some men to reduce the *Kamtschedales* to obedience, which they effected. But by this means a stop was put to the navigation to the river *Anadir*.

In the mean while captain *Pawlutzki*, on the 3d of *September* 1730, arrived at *Anadirskoi Ostrog*. From thence he made, in the following summer, a campaign against the obstinate *Tschuktschi*. I have collected, not only written, but likewise verbal relations of it, from persons who were present on the spot, which are remarkable on account of several circumstances, but especially because they explain the geography of these parts.

The 12th of *March* 1731, *Pawlutzki* marched with 215 *Russians*, 160 *Korjacks*, and 60 *Jukagiri*, against the rebellious *Tschuktschi*. The rout was taken by the sources of the rivers *Uboina*, *Bela*, and *Tscherna*,

Tscherna, which fall in the *Anadir*, and then they turned directly northward to the frozen sea. The source of the river *Anadir* remained to the left of the way. It is not known that they passed any other rivers, since nobody could indicate or name them. After two months, marching hardly more than ten wersts a day, and resting now and then, *Pawlutzki* arrived at the frozen sea, at a place where a considerable river falls into it, which, however, none could name. For a fortnight together he travelled towards the east, along the coasts, mostly upon the ice, without observing the mouths of rivers, because of his going frequently at too great a distance from the land. At last they observed a great company of *Tschuktschi* advancing, who seemed prepared to engage our people. *Pawlutzki*, by his interpreters, summoned them to obedience. But, as they would not listen to it, he attacked them as enemies, and had the good fortune to beat them entirely from the field of battle. This was done on the 7th of *June*.

After eight days rest, *Pawlutzki* went farther, and arrived towards the end of *June* at two rivers, the mouths of which, towards the frozen sea, are about a day's journey distant from each other. On the latter of these rivers a second engagement happened on *June* 30, the event of which was as fortunate as the former.

Hereupon they halted three days, then advanced towards the *Tschukotzkoi Noss*, intending to cross it in their way to the *Anadirsk* sea, when for the third time they met a great army of *Tschuktschi*, who had assembled from from both seas. Here ensued the third engagement, on the 14th of *July*, in which the loss on the side of the enemies was greater than the advantage on the side of the *Russians*; since the *Tschuktschi* would not submit, nor agree to pay tribute among the spoils, some things were found that had belonged to *Schestakow*, the chief of the *Cossacks*, and had been lost in the engagement near the brook *Jegatsch*. Thus they had avenged themselves pretty well of their enemies, since in all the three engagements but three *Russians*, one *Jukagir*, and five *Korjacks*, were killed. We are assured, that among the enemy's slain in the last engagement, there was found one who had two holes in the upper lip on each side of the mouth, through which pieces of sea-horse-teeth are put in.

Now *Pawlutzki* passed in triumph to the *Tschukotzkoi Noss*, he had pretty high mountains to climb, and spent ten days in his way, till he regained the coast. From thence he made part of his people
go

go by water with *baidares*; but he himself with the greatest part of his men, continued upon the land, and followed the coast, which there extends itself towards the south-east, so that every evening he received intelligence from the baidares. The seventh day they came by sea to the mouth of a river, and twelve days after to the mouth of another; upon which, at the distance of about ten wersts, there runs into the sea far towards the east, a point of land, which at first is mountainous, but ends in a plain that cannot be overlooked. This is probably the point of land that caused captain *Bering* to return. Among the mountains upon it, there is one which by the inhabitants of *Anadirskoi Ostrog* is called *Serdze Kamen*. From hence *Pawlutzki* took his rout through the inland country, and came back to *Anadirsk* on the 21st of *October*, by the way he went.

I omit the rest of the exploits of this man of merit, (who afterwards was made a major, then lieutenant-colonel, and at last died at *Jakutzk*, a waywode) and proceed to the second expedition of *Kamtschatka*, which, as it surpasses all those before made, deserves a more circumstantial description.

Captain *Bering* himself made the proposals for it, and he, as well as the two lieutenants, *Spangberg* and *Tschirikow*, declared that they would travel a second time to *Kamtschatka*, and undertake the discoveries that remained to be made in those seas. For this purpose the captain was made a commander, and both lieutenants were raised to be captains in the beginning of the year 1732. The design of the first voyage was not brought on the carpet again upon this occasion, since it was looked upon as compleated; but instead of that, orders were given to make voyages as well eastward to the continent of *America*, as southward to *Japan*, and to discover, if possible, at the same time, through the frozen sea, the north passage, which had been so frequently attempted by the *English* and *Dutch*. The senate, the admiralty-office, and the academy of sciences, all took their parts to compleat this important undertaking, and M. *Kirilow*, the upper secretary in the senate, and afterwards counsellor of state, pushed the affair, so that it was soon brought to bear

The first imperial order from the cabinet to the senate with regard to this affair, was of the 17th of *April* 1732. The senate desired of the academy of sciences, that they might communicate to them the intelligence which till then they had received of *Kamtschatka*,

chatka, and its neighbouring countries, rivers and seas. With this M. *de Lisle* was charged by the academy, and accordingly made a map, upon which *Kamtschatka*, the land of *Jeso*, agreeable to the description of the ship *Castricom*, *Staten Island*, the company's island, *Japan*, and the coast that had been seen by a *Spanish* captain, named, Don *Juan de Gama*, were represented. To this map was added an account in writing, in which M. *de Lisle* described the old discoveries, and proposed ways and means of making new ones. It was therefore after his return to *Paris*, a fault in his memory, to say, in a memoir which he delivered to the academy of sciences at *Paris*, that the said map, and account, had been made by him in the year 1731, and that a new *Kamtschatkan* expedition had been made by it.

When the map and the account belonging to it had been delivered to the senate, by the academy of sciences, there followed an order, that a professor of the academy should be nominated to accompany captain *Bering* in his voyage, who was to ascertain, by astronomical observations, the proper situation of the countries that were to be discovered, and to notice whatever might occur with respect to animals, plants, and minerals belonging to natural history. It happened fortunately for the sciences that two professors of the academy, viz. *John George Gmelin*, professor of chemistry and natural history, and *Lewis de Lisle de la Croyere*, professor of astronomy, voluntarily offered to make the voyage, and, upon the academy's proposal, were nominated by the senate. In the beginning of the year 1733, I myself offered my services, to describe the civil history of *Siberia*, and its antiquities, with the manners and customs of the people, as also the occurrences of the voyage, which was likewise approved of by the senate. It may be said with truth, that so tedious and long a voyage was never undertaken with more alacrity than this was by all who had a share in it.

On account of the several voyages that were to be made, the admiralty ordered the following sea officers to join the commander, as lieutenants: *Peter Laffenius*, *William Walton*, *Dmitri Laptiew*, *Jeger Jendauro*, *Dmitri Owzin*, *Swen Waxel*, *Wasili Prontschischtschew*, *Michailo Plautin*, and *Alexander Scheltinga*, midshipmen. Three of these were designed for the discovery of the north passage, one was to go from the *Ob* to the *Jenisei*,

nisei *, the other out of the *Lena*, towards the west, was likewise to sail into the *Jenisei*, and the third was to sail out of the *Lena* towards the east, round *Tschuketzkoi Nosi*, and to endeavour to reach *Kamtschatka*. The passage from *Archangel* to the *Ob*, the admiralty reserved for their own immediate inspection; for which three lieutenants, *Murawiew*, *Malagin*, and *Skuratow*, were employed. The rest of the sea officers were stationed aboard the ships that were to be commanded by the captain commander, and the captains *Spangberg* and *Tschirikow*. One was also to navigate a particular ship, because it was ordered that four ships should put out to sea from *Kamtschatka*.

Captain *Spangberg* having gone before with a party, and the heaviest materials, on the 21st of *February* 1733, the captain commander set out from *Petersburg* on the 18th of *April*; he went from *Twer* as far as *Casan* by water, and then by *Catherineburg* to *Tobolsk*. The same way was taken by our academical travellers, who departed on the 8th of *August* the same year, and in *January* 1734 overtook the captain commander at *Tobolsk*. The captain commander travelled by the way of *Tara*, *Tomsk*, and *Krasnojarsk*, to *Irkutzk*, from whence he went to the *Lena*, and took advantage of the water carridge as far as *Jakutzk*. On the other hand, captain *Tschirikow* went

---

* *Jenisei* or *Jenzea*. This is one of the largest rivers that runs through *Tartary* and *Siberia*; it extends itself from its source to its mouth, one thousand six hundred *English* miles in length. I could never learn the signification of the name of this great river, the word being neither *Sclavonian* nor *Russian*; nor do the *Tartars*, who live on the banks of it, near its source, give it the name of *Jenisei*, but call it *Kemm*. However, the word *Jenisei* signifying, in the *Tartarian* and *Turkish* tongues, *to swell* or *to over-flow*, and this river overflowing the land every spring, towards its mouth, on both sides, for several miles, it is not unlikely that it had the name *Jenisei* from thence: For *Sai* or *Sei* signifies *Rocky river*, where there are water-falls, and having a rapid current; and *Jenie*, denotes spreading, swelling, *e. g.* the rivers *Jaxartes* and *Cheseldaria*, are also called, near their sources, or *Dsai Dsaibun*: Now the river *Jenisei*, near its springs, between the town of *Abakan* and the river *Kamtschyk*, is not only stony and rocky, but has above ten *Potroggi*, or cataracts; as it has likewise between the cities of *Crosnayabr* and *Jenisei*, not far from *Kenskroi Ostrogg*. Whence it comes, that this river, from the town of *Abakan*, towards its source into *Mungalia*, is not navigable, which otherwise would much shorten and facilitate the way, through *Mungalia* into *China*, and render that trade much more easy as well as profitable. This river, on account of its stony bottom, yields no fish, till below the city of *Jenisei*, and after it has received the rivers *Angara* and *Tungus*, which causes annually a great number of vessels from this city, and others, to go down so far as *Nova Mungaseia*, in order to catch and salt fish. At this city, the river is one werst, or one thousand five hundred paces over; from which the reader may judge of its vast breadth downwards, near the sea, after it has swallowed up so many large rivers.

in

in the summer 1734 from *Tobolsk*, upon the rivers *Irtisch*, *Ob*, *Ret*, *Tunguska* and *Ilim*, as far as *Itimsk*, and only reached *Jakutzk* the following year.

While the ship-building at *Ochotzk* went on, our academical fellow travellers made several tours, that have been of no small advantage to geography and natural history. Professor *de la Croyere* travelled with captain *Tschirikow* by water, left him at the mouth of the river *Ilim*, went farther to *Jakutzk*, and from thence passed the lake *Baical*, to *Selengink*, *Nertschinsk*, and the river *Argun*; but professor *Gmelin* and I went up the *Irtisch*, as far as *Ust-Kamenogorskaia Krepost*; we proceeded farther, by *Koliwano-Woskresenskoi*, *Sawod*, *Kusnetzk*, and *Tomsk*, to *Jeniseisk*; and from thence likewise to the parts situated beyond the lake *Baical*, with which latter voyage we spent the summer of the year 1735. In spring 1736 we assembled again in the upper parts of the river *Lena*. *De la Croyere* went to *Jakutzk*, without staying by the way. *Gmelin* and I spent the whole summer again in this navigation, in order to obtain the more time for our affairs.

The captain commander was still at *Jakutzk*, and from thence took care to transport provisions to *Ochotzk*. Captain *Spangberg* staid with the ship-builders at *Ochotzk*; but both of them had no great success in what they undertook. Every thing went on so slowly, that one could not see when the voyage to *Kamtschatka* would be begun. In the mean while we would not be idle; but were thinking on new travels, in order to employ ourselves. A fire at *Jakutzk* deprived professor *Gmelin* of all his itinerary observations, among which, those he made last summer are particularly to be regretted, (for of the former, copies were already sent to *Petersburg*;) this loss, I say, moved him to go in the summer 1737, up the *Lena* again. But *de la Croyere* made a voyage down the *Lena* to *Schigani Siktak*, and the river *Olenek*. I was obliged, on account of my ill state of health, to accompany M. *Gmelin*, in order to obtain help from him. This sickness was the reason that I did not afterwards return to *Jakutzk*, and there came an order from the senate, which released me from proceeding on the voyage to *Kamtschatka*, and instead of that gave me a commission to travel those countries of *Siberia* where I had not yet been, in order to give a more circumstantial description of all *Siberia*. *Gmelin* petitioned likewise to be recalled, which was granted him. On our being at *Jakutzk* we had

had sent before us to *Kamtschatka*, *Stephen Krascheninikow*, a student, in order to make several preparations there before our arrival. Afterwards, in the year 1738, the *Adjunctus*, *George Wilhelm*, *Steller*, whom the academy of sciences had sent to assist professor *Gmelin*, joined us. By him was compleated what was to be done at *Kamtschatka*, in regard to the sciences.

While the time was spent in preparations for the chief business, several voyages were made along the coasts of the frozen sea, to see whether a passage might not be found that way to *Kamtschatka*. Lieutenant *Murawiew* was first destined for a voyage from *Archangel* to the *Ob*. The first summer, 1734, he got no farther than the river *Petschera*, and wintered at *Pustoserskoi Ostrog*. The following summer he sailed through the streights of *Weygat*, leaving the island of *Weygat* to the left, and the continent to the right. The *Russian* promyschleni, who from *Nova Zembla* go to catch sea-horses, seals, stone-foxes, and white bears, call this passage *Jugorskoi Schar*. The other passage between the island of *Weygat* and *Nova Zembla* was not enquired into. From thence he came again into an open sea, which from a river called *Kara*, that falls into a bay of this sea, bears the name of *Karskoe More*.

Thus far this navigation has been known ever since the beginning of the last century. The inhabitants of *Archangel*, *Kosmagori*, *Meson*, *Pustoserskoi Ostrog*, sail almost annually to *Nova Zembla*, to catch sea-horses, seals, and white bears. There have formerly been voyages made this way by sea to *Siberia*, I mean to the river *Ob*, and to *Mangasea*. This was done in the following manner. *Mutnaja* is the name of a river which with the river *Kara* falls into the same bay. This they sailed up for eight days to a lake, out of which the river has its origin. The lake was crossed in a day. Hereupon the small vessels, or cajucks, that were used for this navigation, were drawn overland 200 fathoms, or according to other accounts 3 Wersts, to another lake, out of which a river known by the name *Selenaia*, or according to the *Russian* Atlas *Tylowka*, runs towards the bay of the river *Ob*. They were obliged to unload these vessels, that they might not be too heavy on account of their being drawn over land, and the goods were carried by land. Now, as this must cost a great deal of labour, especially the drawing of the vessels, several of these vessels commonly join in the passage, that the people may assist one another. Being once in the *Selenaia*, they went with the current, but from the many shallows, almost

most ten days were spent before they reached the bay of the river *Ob*. Then some went to *Obdorskoi Gorodock*, in order to trade with the *Samojades*; but most of them turned into the gulf of the river *Tap*, and thus arrived at the place were formerly stood the town of *Mangasea*.

Along the said cape, Lieut. *Murawiew* sailed in 1735, as far as 72 deg. 30 min. North lat. The Lieutenants *Mlyagin* and *Skuratow* went on with this navigation. They doubled the cape *Jalmal*, and came into the bay of the river *Ob*, so that thereby this navigation may be considered as entirely discovered and accomplished. This was done in the year 1738.

In this same year the navigation from the *Ob* to the river *Jenisei*, with two vessels that were built at *Tobolsk*, was also made by Lieut. *Owzin*, and *Iwan Koschelew*, the master of the fleet. After some difficulties they at last not only happily doubled cape *Matsol*, situated East from the bay of the river *Ob*, but also without farther hindrance entered the *Jenisei*.

Lieut. *Prontschischtschew*, having sailed from *Jakutzk*, on the 27th of *June* 1735, came no farther that summer than to the mouth of the river *Olenek*, where he found a *Russian* village some Werfts up that river, in which he wintered. The following summer he went farther, sailed by the rivers *Anabara*, and *Chatanga*, and did not quite reach the mouth of the river *Taimura*. Here he found a row of islands before him, that extended from the Continent towards the North West, far into the sea. Between them the sea was every were full of ice, and no passage seemed possible. *Prontschischtschew* was of opinion, that if he sailed along the islands he would at last meet with an open sea where these islands end. But this was not the case, he sailed as far as 77 deg. 25 min. North latitude, and found such strong ice before him, that now he gave over all hopes of proceeding farther, and returned and soon after died.

In the year 1738, the lieutenant *Chariton Laptiew* was sent from *Petersburg* in his stead, and had orders, if he could proceed no farther by sea, to describe the coasts by land. In doing of which his travels were of particular use.

Now follows the last voyage into the frozen sea, which was made from the mouth of the river *Lena* towards the east, to discover the way by sea to *Kamtschatka*. It was conducted by lieutenant *Lassenius*. He proceeded on his voyage from *Jakutzk* on the 30th of June

June 1735. On the 7th of *August* he sailed from the mouth of the *Lena*, or properly, from *Buikowskoi Muis*, into the sea; but, on the 14th of the same month, found himself obliged to look out for a harbour to take up his winter quarters, on account of the contrary winds, fogs, and ice. He met with no conveniency for this till the 19th of *August*, on which day this navigation was finished, *Lassenius* then entering the river *Charaulack*, which falls into the frozen sea between the rivers *Lena* and *Jana*. On this river, a werst from its mouth, he met with some old *Jakutzk* habitations. Next to them *Lussenius* had barracks built, with partitions, in which he intended to pass the winter with his people; but he and most of his people were seized with such a dreadful scurvy, that of 52 persons who sailed on board the ship from *Jakutzk* they all died except six men.

Lassenius was succeeded by lieutenant *Dmitri Laptiew*, who, in the beginning of the summer 1736, departed from *Jakutzk* with fresh men. When he came to the river *Charaulack*, where the ship lay; he proceeded on the 15th of *August*, but found, after 48 hours sailing, such rocks of ice before him to the east and north, that he gave up all hopes of proceeding any farther; and, after a consultation had been held, it was unanimously concluded to return to the *Lena*, which he reached on the 23d of *August*, went up the river in the month of *September*, and, on account of the great quantity of ice driving against the vessel, took his winter quarters at the mouth of the little river *Chotuschtack*. Here the scurvy began to appear among the ship's crew; but a stop was put to the progress of the distemper by the leaves or points of the dwarf cedar, which grows there, and, according to the custom of that country, by frozen fish, which, raw and frozen as they are, are scraped small and eaten. By this food, added to assiduous labour and exercise, most of the men preserved their health, and the sick were restored.

Our academical fellow-travellers were at *Jakutzk*, when, in the beginning of the year 1737, advice was received there from lieutenant *Laptiew*, of this navigation having miscarried now the second time. The instructions given by the senate to the captain commander contained, that if such a navigation could not be accomplished in the first voyage, it was to be attempted a second time; and if, even then, they should meet with obstacles, the commanding officer should be sent to *Petersburgh* to give an account of his

voyages

voyages to the senate and admiralty. Now two voyages had been made in vain, of which, however, lieutenant *Laptiew* had made but one, so that the captain commander was undetermined what to do. His instructions likewise directed him to advise with the professors that were in the *Kamtschatkan* expedition. This was done. His and our judgment was, that the decision should be left to the senate. At that time I had already gathered from the archieves of *Jakutzk*, those intelligences of former navigations through the frozen sea, some of which I have inserted in the beginning of this tract. I digested them in proper order, and added other accounts of the present nature of the frozen sea, which I had likewise learned at *Jakutzk* from persons who had been in that sea. Now, to promote a common good thereby, in case any farther attempt should be made, I delivered my writings to the captain commander, who sent them to *Petersburgh*, where, in 1742, they were inserted in the *Petersburgh* observations, by way of extracts.

In consequence of this, the captain commander sent an order to the lieutenant *Laptiew* to return with the boat *Irkutzk*, and all the men, to *Jakutzk*. He came, and travelled to *Petersburgh*, from whence, in 1738, he was again dispatched to *Siberia*. Another attempt was to be made, whether the navigation, which, according to the accounts discovered by me, had been really accomplished many years ago, might not possibly be made now. In case the lieutenant should meet with unsurmountable difficulties, he was ordered to follow the coast by land, and to make both a circumstantial description of them, and a chart. It must be owned that this able and industrious officer has spared no pains to fulfil the orders he had received, though he did not every where meet with the success he could have wished. He arrived in the spring 1739 at the first open water at *Jakutzk*, embarked on board his former ship, and sailed in her towards the frozen sea. On the 15th of *August* he came to the *Swjatoi Noss*, and at the end of the mouth to the mouths of the *Indigirka*. Here was already such a severe winter, that the ship was frozen in on the 1st of *September*. *Laptiew* would have entered one of the mouths of this river, had not they been too shallow for his ship. A storm tore the vessel loose, and drove her farther into the sea, where, on the 9th of *September*, he was frozen in again about 60 wersts from the land. The men had now no other resource

but bringing the naval stores and provisions ashore, which was effected, and the ship itself, as it could not be avoided, was left to her fate. *Laptiew* having passed the winter on the river *Indigirka*, went the following summer in a small vessel along the coast to the river *Kolyma*; for to follow the coasts any farther, either by land or by water was not adviseable, on account of the *Tschuktschi*: he therefore went over land to *Anadirsk*, and from thence as far as the mouth of the river *Anadir*. Here his expedition was finished, after which no other has been undertaken through the frozen sea in those parts.

The use of all these endeavours was, on the one hand, to afford an increase of knowledge, and more certainty in the geography of those parts, and, on the other, to ascertain, in the most decisive manner, the impossibility of the navigation through the frozen sea, that had been formerly undertaken by the *English* and *Dutch*, in order to discover a nearer way to the *East Indies*, which has here been so artfully done, that now, in my opinion, nobody will easily think of attempting any such voyage. To put this important truth in its full light, I will add the following considerations:

First, such a navigation ought to be made in one summer, if it be of any use. But now we have seen, that we cannot get in one summer so much as from *Archangel* to the *Ob*, and from thence to the *Jenisei*. Five or six years have elapsed before one such single voyage was accomplished. And have not also the *Dutch* and *English* met with infinite difficulties in their passage through the streights *Weygat*?

In the next place, between the *Pjasida* and *Chatanga*, a row of islands extends from the continent a great way into the sea, and denies all passage as well on one side as the other. *Jelmerland* is represented by *Hasius*, in his map of *Russia*, discovered in 1664, according to ancient accounts, uniting *Nova Zembla* to *Siberia*. These islands may be the same impediment to navigation.

The same may be said of the vast rocks of ice to be met with, that are firmly fixed. These, at the same time, raise a doubt against the opinion of those who are for ordering a navigation, not along the coasts, but through the wide sea, near the north pole. 'Tis true, the voyage would be much shorter; but would not the obstructions remain the very same? For, if the before-mentioned mountains of ice, such as have been found about *Greenland* and *Spitzbergen*,

bergen, are innumerable, there must then be something that hinders the motion that would otherwise be communicated to them by the sea and the winds. This may be occasioned by the ice being continued as far as the north pole, or because under the pole, or near it, there is land to which the mountains of ice are fixed at the bottom, since they are deeper under the water than above it. Capt. *Wood*, in 1676, strongly maintained the probability of the north passage, near the north pole, before he commenced that voyage; but by the voyage itself he was sufficiently convinced of the impossibility of it.

It is true, in the description of the most ancient navigations through the frozen sea, I have no where, with certainty, found that great country which has been reported to be situated in the frozen sea: but this is no proof that it does not exist. The *American* coast lying opposite the land of the *Tschuktschi*, may extend far enough to the north and west, without our knowing it. And if so, it would, together with the mountains of ice fixed to it, be directly in the way of those who would pass by it near the north pole.

Even the passage along the coasts does not promise better success than that with which it was made 100 years ago. The general observation that the water in the sea decreases, proves also here true. There is to be seen along the coasts of the frozen sea, wood cast on shore on such heights that now-a-days are not to be reached by any flood or waves. Not far from the mouth of the river *Jana*, in the west, there is said to lie an old *Koschi*, remote from the sea shore now about five wersts. From this, an extraordinary flatness of the coast is to be concluded, which is also confirmed by verbal relations of people who have frequently been at the frozen sea. But such a change is by no means advantageous for the navigation, which is mostly made in a channel, not very wide, between the ice and the continent, which grows shallower and shallower. In the year 1709 it was hardly possible to go with schitikes between the rivers *Indigirka* and *Kolyma*, though these vessels are smaller than the kotitches formerly, and do not go so deep, of which I have a written testimony. Now, if still smaller and flatter vessels were built, they would do very well for such shallow places: but, as in some places there are likewise steep rocks that project into the sea, they would do the less service there; not to mention that small vessels are intirely contrary to the intention of the voyage.

In

In the like manner there are impediments which particularly foreign ships would meet with, were they to undertake this passage. When, in our days, the navigations through the frozen sea were to be made, people were sent out from all the rivers falling into the frozen sea, who were obliged to erect at the mouths, certain marks, by piling up wood, for the navigators to direct their course by, at their arrival in those parts. Magazines were established in several places along the coasts, out of which, in case of need, the provisions might be taken. All the Pagan nations, dwelling thereabouts, were apprized of the navigation, and had orders, on the first call, to hasten to the assistance of the mariners. Such advantages no foreign ships can promise themselves. They must always put a wonderful confidence in their own strength, which, however, may too easily fail. What they do not bring with them, they must not expect to find; and, supposing it was to be hoped that the natives there would not deny foreign ships their assistance, yet they are but seldom to be met with along the sea coasts, but rather go up the rivers, because there they enjoy greater advantages of hunting.

And what sad consequences attend an *European* ship, (like *Heemskirk* at *Nova Zembla*) being obliged to winter there? The manner of living, and food of the *European* mariners, are by no means fit for such winter quarters. Brandy, salt meat, and biscuit, are no remedies against the scurvy; and the want of exercise, which necessarily follows, when a sailor has nothing to do out of his hut, is still more fatal.

In such cases the manner of living of the *Russians* may serve for a pattern, they almost every other year alternately winter at *Nova Zembla*, without any harm. These imitate the *Samojedes* in drinking frequently the fresh blood of rain-deer. The brandy, of which they make provision for the voyage, they consume before they reach the coast of *Nova Zembla*. They know nothing of salt, or dry victuals, but live upon the fresh game which they catch, especially on wild rain-deer. Hunting requires continual motion. No body remains there above one day at a time in his hut, except he is hindered from going out by too great a storm, or too much snow. Not to mention, that these people are provided with good warm furr'd cloaths, which the *European* sailors want. These are, in my opinion, reasons sufficient to prevent any nation's undertaking for the

future such an enterprise. Father *Castel* * had the same opinions before; but then they were without sufficient foundation, and men would have remained in a continual uncertainty, if the above related navigation through the frozen sea had not cleared up the matter.

We proceed now to the chief business of the second *Kamtschatka* expedition, which consisted in the navigations that were to be made from *Ochotzk* and *Kamtschatka* to the East and South. Capt. *Spangberg* was already in the month of *June* 1734 arrived at *Jakutzk*, and had prosecuted the voyage, on the rivers *Aldan*, *Maia*, and *Judoma*, with the vessel, of which till then he had made use of, in order to reach, if possible, before the winter, *Judomskoi Krest*. But he was frozen in, above 150 Wersts from the place, and advanced on foot with a few men to *Judomskoi Krest*, and *Ochotzk*. Now, that he might not want there what was most necessary, the captain commander sent there, in the spring of 1735, an hundred horses, every one loaded with five pouds of meal, according to the custom of the country. In the next place, they were endeavouring to transport from *Jakutzk* to *Judomskoi Krest*, the naval stores and provisions in vessels that were partly arrived with the captain commander, and partly built at *Jakutzk*, and at the mouth of the river *Maja*. In the summer 1736, Capt. *Tschirikow* had the inspection of them, and went the subsequent winter to *Ochotzk*. In the summer 1737, lieutenant *Wavel* transmitted 33000 pouds of provisions and materials by the same road to *Judomskoi Krest*; but from *Judomskoi Krest* the transport was made in winter by land, to the river *Urak*, where magazines were established, new vessels built, and the stores were removed to *Ochotzk*, with the first open water, when this river, which, in summer, is very shallow, swelled very much. The place, on the upper part of the river *Urak*, from whence the vessels put off, was called *Uratzkoe Plotbijchtsche*; it lies about half way between *Judomskoi Krest* and *Ochtzk*; but the river comprehends, with its windings to the sea, about 200 Wersts, which may be accomplished in seventeen hours, without oars, by means of the swift current.

In the mean while, Capt. *Spangberg* had ordered two vessels to be built at *Ochotzk*, for the voyage he was commanded to make to *Japan*; an hucker, named *Michael the Archangel*, and a double shallop, called the *Hope*. These were quite finished at the end of the summer, 1737.

* *Dissertation sur la celebre Terre de* Kamtschatka, *et sur celle d'Yeco dans les Memoires de Treveux* 1737, Juillet. p. 1169.

Bering, the captain commander, who, in the same summer, came to *Ochotzk*, had two more packet boats for the *American* voyage, and two vessels for provisions built, that were only to serve as far as *Kamtschatka*. All these were finished in the summer 1740, and the two packet boats were called by the names of *St Peter*, and *St Paul*. In the mean time they went on without interruption, transporting the provisions from *Jakutzk* to *Judomskoi Krest*, and from thence to *Ochotzk*. A great help towards which was, that, upon the representation of the captain commander, two lieutenants of the fleet, *Wasilei Larionew*, and *Gabriel Tolbuchin*, were, in 1738, sent by the admiralty to *Siberia*, the first of whom provided at *Jakutzk*, and the second at *Irkutzk*, whatever was necessary for the *Kamtschatka* expedition.

In consequence of this, they were able to make a beginning with the navigation to *Japan*, in 1738, Capt. *Spangberg* commanded the hucker *Michael*, and Lieut. *Walton*, the double shallop, called the *Hope*. The boat *Gabriel* of the first *Kamtschatka* voyage, was added to them, and the command of her intrusted to the midshipman *Scheltinga*; with these three vessels Capt. *Spangberg* set sail from *Ochotzk*, about the middle of *June* 1738. Sooner he could not sail, for till that time the sea was full of ice, and he had even then much trouble in getting through it. He steered first towards *Kamtschatka*, entered the river *Bolschaia-reka*, and made preparations for his future winter quarters. After a short stay there, he directed his course to the *Kurilian* islands, and arrived at them by a South and West course, in 46 deg. N. Lat. in the beginning of autumn, but returned to *Kamtschatka*, with intent to put out to sea earlier the following summer, and then to end the navigation. During his winter residence, Capt. *Spangberg* built at *Bolscheretzkoi Ostrog*, a small yacht, a decked shallop, of birch wood, with twenty four oars, which he called *Bolschaia-reka*, to make use of it the better to discover the islands, in case the hucker and double shallop could be of no service between those islands.

On *May* 22, 1739, the navigation was began again, with all the four vessels; they waited for one another at the first *Kurilian* islands, where the captain gave the officers under him the necessary instructions, and the signals were agreed upon. This being done, they proceeded on their voyage, on the 1st of *June*, steering South East, till about 47 deg. North Lat. without meeting with any land, and then S. W. in order to reach again the *Kurilian* islands, which they did. On the

the 14th of *June*, there was a violent storm, with a very thick fog, in which Lieut. *Walton*, with the double shallop, was separated from Capt. *Spangberg*, and, tho' they sought each other for two days, and fired several guns for signals, yet they did not join again during the voyage. Each therefore made his navigation for himself; they both landed in *Japan* at different places, and, after their return, gave the following accounts to the captain commander.

Capt. *Spangberg* came to an anchor under the land of *Japan*, on the 18th of *June*, in 25 fathom water, accounting it to be in 38 deg. 41 min. N. Lat. A multitude of *Japannese* vessels were seen, as also some valleys on the shore, at a distance were pretty high woods. Two *Japannese* vessels came rowing towards them, which, at 30 or 40 fathoms distance, stopped, and would not approach nearer. When the men on board the ship beckoned for them to come up, they did the same, and made them understand that the captain and his people should go on shore. But this Capt. *Spangberg* carefully avoided, nay, he did not long remain in one place, for fear of being surprized.

On the 20th of *June*. many *Japannese* vessels were again seen, each of which contained ten or twelve men. On the 22d. the captain anchored at another place, in 38 deg. 25 min. N. Lat. there two fishing boats came on board, and the men exchanged fresh fish, rice, large tobacco leaves, pickled cucumbers, and other things, for various *Russian* goods, with which the ship's company were provided. Cloth, and cloaths made of cloth, likewise bits of blue glass, seemed most agreeable to tne *Japannese*, but they did not set any value on cotten, and silk stuffs, nor on looking glasses, scissars, needles, and such like implements, that were shewn them, having all these in their own country. They were very civil, and reasonable in their prices.

The ship's company got of them some oblong square gold coin, of the same kind as are described and represented by *Kæmpfer*; they are not of so high a colour as the *Dutch* ducats, and somewhat lighter, as I have found by examining one of them, and observed, by comparing it to a *Dutch* ducat, the difference in weight to be two grains.

The following day, seventy nine such fishing boats were seen at a distance, all of which were flat at the stern, and sharp at the head. Their breadth was from four and a half to five feet, and their length about twenty four feet, in the midst was a deck, and upon it a small hearth, the rudder might be taken out, and put in the vesssel when not used: Some vessels had two rudders, both behind, one on each side,

but

but bent quite crooked. They use their oars standing. They are also provided with four hooked small anchors.

They use another kind of vessels to trade to the circumjacent islands, and even at a great distance along the coast. These are much larger than the former, sharp equally at the head and the stern; they carry more people, and sail better, though chiefly before the wind; but they are easily cast away by contrary winds and weather, when the people, on account of their inexperience in navigation, do not know how to help themselves, but submit to their fate. Such were those cast away on the coast of *Kamtschatka*.

The *Japannese* are mostly of a small stature, and of a swarthy complexion, with black eyes, and flat noses. The men, and great boys, shave their hair from the forehead to the crown, the rest of the hair is combed smooth, and made to shine with glue; it is tied in the neck behind, and wrapped up in a paper. From these little boys are distinguished by a shaved patch in the middle of the crown, one and a half, or two inches over, about which the rest of their hair is dressed in the same manner as that of the former; their cloaths are long and wide, after the manner of the *European* nightgowns; they do not wear breeches, but, instead of them, the lower part of their bodies is wrapped up in linnen.

Before Capt. *Spangberg* left this place, a great canoe came to his ship, in which, besides the mariners, sat four men, who, if we may judge from their embroidered cloaths, and appearance in other respects, seemed to be people of condition. The Captain invited them into his cabin; at going in they bowed down to the ground, held up their hands folded over their heads, and kneeled till the Captain desired them to rise; they were entertained with brandy and eatables, which they seemed to like. When the Captain shewed them a chart of those parts, and also a globe, they immediately knew their country, the name of which they pronounced *Niphon*. They likewise pointed out with their fingers, on the chart, the islands *Matsmai* and *Sado*, and also the capes *Songar* and *Noto*. At parting, they again bowed to the ground, and expressed their thanks, as well as they could, for what they had received; the same day, the former fishing boats came again, and brought several things for sale, which they exchanged for *Russian* goods.

Capt. *Spangberg* had now no doubt that the chief design of his voyage, which was the discovery of the proper situation of *Japan*,

with

with respect to the country of *Kamtschatka*, was fulfilled. Therefore, some days after, he set out on his return, wherein he made several observations on the islands he had seen before, and by which he was obliged to pass again. I cannot avoid mentioning his observations, referring for the rest to the map he has made of this voyage, contained in the *Russian* Atlas.

He sailed to the N. E. and arrived on the 3d of *July*, in lat. 43 deg. 50 min. at a great island, before which he anchored in 30 fathoms water, and sent his birch yatch with a boat on shore, in search of fresh water; but they could find no landing place, on account of the steep rocks, of which the coast consisted. He therefore sailed to another place, from whence the boat was again sent ashore, and brought 13 casks of good water on board. On this island grew birch, firs, and other trees, unknown to the *Russian* sailors; they saw men, who ran away as soon as they perceived the *Russians*; they found leathern boats, and the bottom covering, or soles of sledges, made after the *Kurilian* and *Kamtschatkan* manner. This induced the Captain to sail nearer, and to come to an anchor in a sandy bottom in a bay, at eight fathoms water. By this bay was a village, to which the Captain sent a shallop, that brought eight of the inhabitants on board.

The aspect and stature of those people were like those of the *Kuriles*, and they speak the same language. One chief difference between them consisted in this, that they had pretty long hair all over their bodies; the men of a middling age had black, and the old had grey beards, some of them wore silver ear-rings. Their cloaths were made of silk stuffs of various colours, and reached to their feet, which were bare. They had brandy given them, and presents were made them of various trifles, which they thankfully received. Seeing a live cock on board the ship, they fell upon their knees, clapped their hands together over their heads, and bowed down to the ground, both before the cock, and for the presents they had received. After which the Captain set them ashore.

On the 9th of *July*, Capt. *Spangberg* left this island, and sailed to discover the situation of the others in its neighbourhood, in order to insert them with certainty in his map. This was not done without danger and inconvenience. Sometimes they had only from three to four or five fathoms water, many of the ship's company grew sick, and several died soon after. On the 23d of *July*, he arrived by a South West coast in 41 deg. 22 min. North lat. at the island *Matsmai*,

mai, where he found three large *Japannese* busses, on which account he prepared for an engagement, in case they should attack him, and was so cautious that he would neither send ashore, nor come to an anchor; but, on the 25th, set sail on his return to *Kamtschatka*. On the 15th of *August* he reached the mouth of the river *Bolschaia-reka*, which he entered in order to give his people a little rest. On the 20th he set sail again. On his return to *Ochotzk*, on the 29th, he found Lieut. *Walton* already there, from whose report I shall now mention what is most remarkable.

Walton having been separated in a fog and tempest, from Capt. *Spangberg*, whom he endeavoured in vain to rejoin, took the resolution to seek, without loss of time, the land of *Japan*, of which he got sight two days after, viz. on the 16th, in 38 deg. 17 min. North lat. According to his account, he was then from the first *Kurilian* island, 11 deg. 45 min. variation. He sailed farther to the South, to 33 deg. 48 min. North lat. following mostly the coasts, and made the following observations: On the 17th of *June*, being near the shore, 39 *Japannese* vessels of the size of gallies appeared, seeming to come out of a harbour; but soon separated for different places. They had straight sails of cotton stuffs, some blue and white striped, others all white. *Walton* pursued one of them in search of a harbour, and arrived before a great town or city, where he anchored in 30 fathoms water. On the 19th, a *Japannese* vessel, with 18 persons on board, came to the *Russian* ship. As the people appeared very civil, and by tokens gave them to understand that they might come on shore, the lieutenant sent the second mate *Lew Kasimerow*, and the quarter master *Tscherkaschenin*, with six armed soldiers in a yawl ashore, and gave them two empty casks, which they were to fill with fresh water. He provided them, at the same time, with things of which they were to make presents to the *Japannese*, in order to gain their friendship.

When these approached the shore, above 100 small vessels came to meet them, and crowded so hard upon the yawl, that they could scarce use their oars. The *Japannese* rowers were naked to the girdle. They shewed pieces of gold, of which they had not a small quantity, as a token, seemingly, that they had a mind to engage in trade with their foreign guests. Mean while, the yawl landed, and the small vessel stayed behind at some distance. On the shore were assembled an innumerable multitude of people, they all bowed to
the

the new comers. The two empty water-casks were carried ashore by the *Japannese* with great complaisance, filled with water, and brought back into the yawl.

During this interval, the second mate and the quarter master with four soldiers went on shore, leaving two soldiers as a guardian in the yawl. The town consisted of about 1500 wooden and stone houses, which took a space of about three werfts along the coast. *Kasimerow* went into the houses, in which he saw that his casks were carried. At the door he was received by the landlord in an extraordinary friendly manner, conducted into an apartment, and entertained with wine and deserts, which were both served in porcelain vessels. The desert consisted in grapes, apples, oranges, and preserved radishes. Out of this house he went into another, where he was treated in the same manner, and, besides, had boiled rice presented him to eat. The same was done to the quarter master, and soldiers that were with him. *Kasimerow*, on his part, presented his benefactors, and the people who took care of his casks, with glass beads, and other trifles. After this, he patroled the town a little, and observed every where, as well in the houses as streets, a great deal of cleanliness and good order. In some houses he met with shops, where chiefly, cotton stuffs were sold. In this hurry they did not observe any silk stuffs. Horses, cows, and hens, he found in abundance. The fruits of the field there consisted in wheat and pease.

When *Kasimerow* returned to his yawl again, he saw before him two men with sabres, and one had two sabres in his hands. This filled him with some apprehensions, wherefore he hurried to the ship as fast as he could.

Above one hundred small *Japannese* vessels, with 15 men in each, followed the yawls to observe the ship near at hand. In one of them was a gentleman, who ordered a rope to be thrown into the yawls to have his small vessel drawn quite near the ship. He came on board; by his fine silk cloaths, and the respect that was shewed him by his retinue, it was judged he was the governor of the place. He made a present to Lieut. *Waln* of a vessel with wine, which the latter brought with him to *Ochotzk*. The wine was of a dark-brown colour, pretty strong, and not disagreeable of taste, only somewhat tart. But it might perhaps be damaged by the heat at sea. These civilities the Lieutenant returned by other presents. He treated,

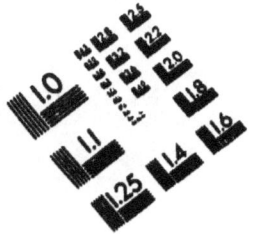

**IMAGE EVALUATION
TEST TARGET (MT-3)**

Photographic
Sciences
Corporation

23 WEST MAIN STREET
WEBSTER, N.Y. 14580
(716) 872-4503

ed, moreover, his guest and his retinue with victuals and drink, when it was observed, that the *Japannese* did not find the taste of the *Russian* brandy amiss. At the same time the ship's crew carried on a little trade with the *Russians*. Whatever the latter had, even old shirts, stockings, &c. the *Japannese* liked. They paid for them in their copper coin, which, as that of the *Chinese*, has a square hole in the middle, and is strung together. At last the person of quality, with demonstrations of satisfaction and gratitude, returned to the town. In the mean time *Walton* observed, that the many small vessels which surrounded his ship, continually increased, and, therefore, thinking himself not safe, weighed anchor and put to sea again, having first fired a gun in token of his taking leave.

The 22d of *June* he reached land again, and anchored in 23 fathoms water. The anchor did not hold, and they were obliged to weigh it again. They looked about for a more convenient landing place, but the coast was every where steep and rocky. In one place vessels were observed, which, though not small, were drawn ashore for want of an harbour. *Walton* therefore returned to the place, where, before, he could not succeed in anchoring, when some small vessels came to his assistance; he gave them to understand that he was in want of water. Immediately the *Japannese* took the casks, that were given them, went ashore with them, and returned them full of fresh water. They also shewed our people a written paper, which was taken for an order, by virtue of which they are obliged to give all assistance to strangers. It seemed as if the *Japannese* wanted to give the Lieutenant to understand to come nearer to the shore, where there was a harbour into which the ship might be hauled; and that they would help him in it. But before *Walton* resolved upon it, a boat came from the shore, which forbid the people any further communication. In the boat was a person who was taken for a soldier, having a sword by his side, and a pistol in his hand. On which Lieutenant *Walton* supposed this to be a *Japannese* guard-boat.

The next day they came to an anchor in another place near the shore, in two fathoms water, where the ground consisted in a coarse sand and muscle-shells. Considering the great heat of the summer, they could not lay in too much fresh water; and besides this furnished always new opportunities to get intelligence about the country. Wherefore *Walton* sent the 24th of *June*, the second gunner, *Jurje Alexan-*

Alexandrow, with some men, and a surgeon's apprentice, named *Iwan Djagilew*, in the yawl on shore. *Alexandrow* found no water, but saw *Japannese*, who were clad in long white linnen frocks. The horses in this country were of a dark brown and black colour. He brought back with him an orange tree, pearl-shells, and the branch of a pine-tree. But the apprentice gathered herbs, and especially provided himself with the buds of the fir-tree, of which afterwards they made decoction, for the sick on board the ship.

Now *Walton* having sailed about the coasts of *Japan* a while longer, and having made a passage pretty far to the East, to see whether he could not discover any land, or islands there, which however was not effected, he returned to *Kamtschatka*, and arrived the 23d of *July*, on the river of *Bolschaia-reka*, where he tarried till the 7th of *August*, to join, if possible, Capt. *Spangberg*. But as, in the mean time, the latter did not arrive, he proceeded on his voyage to *Ochotzk*, which he reached the 21st of *August*.

It is not necessary to make particular mention of the third vessel, commanded by the midshipman *Scheltinga*, he having had the same fate with the captain, from whom he was not separated during the voyage. *Spangberg*, as well as *Walton*, have made charts of their navigations, from which those are composed that are inserted in the *Russian* Atlas.

After his arrival, Capt. *Spangberg* obtained permission from the captain commander to winter at *Jakutzk*, and then to travel to *Petersburg*, in order to give an account himself of his expedition to the senate and admiralty. Mean time advice was sent to *Petersburg* of the discoveries made by him. Now, although at first they were well received, and occasioned the order of the captain commander, about Capt. *Spangberg*'s return to *Petersburg* to be confirmed, yet the opinions soon changed. The proofs of *Spangberg*'s having been in *Japan*, were looked upon as not convincing enough. *Kirilow*'s general map of *Russia*, after the example of *Strahlenberg*'s, represented *Japan* almost under the same meridian with *Kamtschatka*. Whereas, according to the course and observations of *Spangberg*, and *Walton*, it ought to lie 11 or 12 degrees more to the Westward. It was believed *Spangberg* might have mistaken the coasts of *Korea* for *Japan*: And it was thought proper that he should attempt a second navigation, and that, in this expedition, he should have for interpreters two *Russian* lads, who had learnt the *Japannese* language of the *Japannese* that come to *Petersburg*, in the year 1732.

This order *Spangberg* obtained at *Kirenskoi Ostrog*, in the month of *July* 1740, being already on his travels to *Petersburg*. He went back to *Jakutzk*, and from thence to *Ochotzk*, where he did but just see the captain commander, because every thing was now ready for his intended voyage. In the mean while the proper season for the voyage to *Japan* was not only past for this year, but a vessel was likewise wanting, since, one of those which *Spangberg* had used, in his first voyage, was sent to *Kamtschatka*, by the captain commander, on account of certain preparations. It was therefore necessary to build a new one, and that was done the following winter under *Spangberg*'s inspection, who resided at *Ochotzk* till the vessel was compleated.

In the summer 1741, he went to sea with her, but she soon became leaky, so that they could scarce reach the coasts of *Kamtschatka*. The reason of it was ascribed to the hasty building of the vessel, and the wood having had no time to dry. The refitting of her, at the mouth of the river *Bolschaia-reka*, and *Spangberg*'s passing the winter, for this reason, at *Bolscheretzkoi Ostrog* was to no purpose: For he having set sail again the 25th of *May* 1742, and being hardly passed the first *Kurilian* islands, the water got into her again without his being able to prevent it, or to stop the leaks. In this situation of affairs *Spangberg* did not choose to return without having made any discoveries at all. He sent out the midshipman *Scheltinga* to discover the parts of the sea as far as the mouth of the river *Amur*, but also this had not the wished for success. In short, the whole second voyage of Capt. *Spangberg* was nothing but a series of adversities.

Thus ended the navigation to *Japan*. By degrees the arguments increased that our sailors had not missed the aim the first time. And now no body doubts any more of it, since the most famous *French* geographers, such as *d'Anville*, *Buache*, and *Bellin*, admit in their maps as great, nay, a somewhat greater difference of longitude between *Kamtschatka* and *Japan*, than *Spangberg* and *Walton*.

The expedition of Capt. *Spangberg* to *Japan* in the year 1738, had deprived the chief detachment at *Ochotzk* in such a manner of provision, that two years elapsed before it was sufficiently supplied again by fresh importations. During which time also two new vessels were built at *Ochotzk*, viz. the packet-boats *St Peter* and *St Paul*, which were properly designed for the intended *American* discoveries. The captain commander had sent before him to *Kamtschatka*, in autumn 1739, the pilot *Iwan Jelagin*, with one of the vessels that had been with Capt. *Spangberg*, in order to enquire into the bay of *Awatscha*, on the east coast of that country, where all the requisite conveniencies for a harbour were reported to be, and to establish magazines and build barracks there. In the following spring 1740, the professors, *De Lisle de la Croyere*, and the Adjunctus *Steller*, arrived at *Ochotzk*, and from *Petersburgh*, the lieutenant of the fleet *Iwan Tschichatschew*, and the master of the fleet *Sophron Chitrow*, who soon after was made a lieutenant, these latter were to supply the places of other sick and discharged officers.

Now, nothing more being wanting, it was resolved to pass over to *Kamtschatka* in the same summer. But the departure was delayed till the 4th of *September*. The captain commander conducted the packet-boat *St Peter*, and Capt. *Tschirikow* the packet-boat *St Paul*. Two other ships were loaded with provisions, and *De la Croyere* and *Steller* had a particular vessel for their stores, with which they followed the rest of this small squadron the 8th of *September*, when the packet-boats arrived at the mouth of the river *Bolschaia-reka*, the 20th of *September*, the captain commander ordered the store ships to enter it. *De la Croyere's* and *Steller's* voyage was finished here, because they had proposed to make observations and discoveries at *Bolscheretzkoi Ostrog*; but the captain commander and captain *Tschirikow*, finding the entrance into the river too shallow for their ships, went the next day farther, and doubling the South point of *Kamtschatka*, made the harbour *Awatscha*.

In passing the streights between this point and the first *Kurilian* islands, the captain commander perceived, by the danger he found himself in, how necessary the precaution had been of his leaving behind him the store ships at *Bolschaia-reka*. In the midst of the streights, which is reckoned three leagues broad and one league long, there lies a great ridge of rocks, over which the water rolls. It is passable on both sides, but the South passage being broader is preferable to that on the North side. Favourable and strong as the wind was with which the captain commander thought to pass the streight, it little availed, since just, at that very time, he had a strong flood against him, and, being unacquainted with these seas, he had never seen such a one before. For an hour together it could not be observed on the coasts that the ship had advanced in the least. The waves,

waves, which were very high, beat over the ship's stern, and a boat that was tied to the ship, with a rope of forty fathoms long, often beat against the ship with great violence, nay, once it had almost been flung on board with the waves. We had from ten to twelve fathoms water, but when the ship with the waves went down, she was reckoned to be hardly three fathoms from the ground. The wind was so vehement that they could only carry the fore-sail and top-sail, and nothing was to be done but to keep the ship steady before the wind, against the flood, for had they turned her ever so little, they would have been in danger from the waves. Besides the aforesaid ridge of rocks was very near, which they had reason to be afraid of, and carefully to avoid, least they should be wrecked upon it. When the vehement of the flood began somewhat to abate, the ship advanced by little and little, and being quite passed the streights, they at last saw themselves free from all farther impediments. This only happened to the captain commander, whereas *Tschirikow*, passing through an hour and a half later, met with no difficulties.

It was on the 26th of *September* when they passed the said streights. The following day they arrived before the bay of *Awatscha*; but a thick fog just rising, hindered them from discerning the entrance, they were obliged to put to sea again. Finally, both packet-boats had the good luck to enter the bay and harbour of *Awatscha*, on the 8th of *October*, where they spent the following winter.

This bay has its name from the river *Awatscha*, or properly, according to *Kamtschadalian* pronunciation, *Suaatscha*, and empties itself into the bay from the West side. This latter is almost circular, and about twenty Wersts diameter. The entrance may be from 3 to 400 fathoms broad, extends to the Southward, and is so deep that the large ships may sail through it. The bay itself is also of a good depth. Three natural divisions in the bay were all alike convenient for harbours, viz. *Niakina*, *Kakowaia*, and *Tareinaia-guba*, and were only distinguished in largeness. The pilot *Jelagin* had chosen the first and least for a harbour for the packet-boats, and near it built magazines, houses, and barracks, and named it *Petropaulowska*, or the harbour of *St Peter* and *St Paul*.

An officer, who during forty years had navigated the seas to all parts of the universe, and was now in this expedition, gave this harbour the character of being the best place for shipping that ever he had seen. It will hold twenty ships conveniently, is covered from all winds, has a sandy ground, and from 14 to 18 feet water; so that larger vessels than packet-boats may lie in it. There is, moreover, very good and wholesome water found in the neighbourhood, particularly that of the river *Awatscha*, which is much preferred before the water of some rivers and brooks thereabouts, that have their origin out of morasses. From the entrance of the bay to the harbour, one steers N. N. W. and N. W. by N. where there is 8, 9, 10 and 11 fathoms water, and a secure passage over sandy ground, except about 3 Wersts before the harbour, where in the middle of the channel there lies several sunk stones, of which one must be cautious, as there is but eight feet of water. The highest water there, at the time of the new or full moon, when the spring tides happen, is five feet eight inches *English* measure, according to observations that have been made for that purpose.

During the winter quarters at *Petropawlowska*, all endeavours were used to get transported hither the provisions that were brought to *Bolscheretzkoi*; but that could not be quite compleated. The distance between both places is 212 Wersts. As, in *Kamtschatka*, there are no horses, they were not only obliged to put dogs to the carriages, but to fetch these creatures sometimes at the distance of four or five hundred Wersts; eight or ten times as many dogs were required as they would have wanted horses; for the horses in *Russia* draw in winter time, where the roads are bad, forty pouds, for which weight eight or ten dogs are necessary in *Kamtschatka*. The *Kamtschedales* were not used to such relays, especially at so great a distance from their habitations; so that it occasions many hindrances. But they had been aware of this, and therefore had bought up a good number of raindeer at *Anadirskoi Ostrog*, and drove them to *Awatscha*, where they had a good pasture, and were consumed during the following winter; they likewise got dried fish in abundance of the *Kamtschedales*, so that half of the usual sea provision could be saved. But, in the following spring 1741, the captain commander ordered one of the ships, that remained behind at *Bolscheretzkoi*, to bring over the rest of the provisions that were left there, she arrived happily in the harbour of *Petropawlowska*, before he put to sea, and delivered her cargo, partly on board the ships that were ready to sail, and partly into the magazines there.

When the roads began to grow better, *De la Croyere* and *Steller* arrived at *Petropawlowska*, to assist at the the intended *American* discoveries

coveries. The captain commander took with him the latter, and the first joined *Tschirikow*.

Now the question was, what course they should steer in their voyage? To determine which, the captain commander, on the 4th of *May*, called all the officers together to hold a council, to which also the Professor *De la Croyere* was invited. Every one was to give his opinion, out of which the best was to be chosen. Now the indications of a near country towards the East were known to every one, and the officers had judged, during the whole winter, that the coast must be kept towards the East, or somewhat Northerly. But with this *de Lisle*'s map did not agree, of which I have mentioned above, that it had been presented by the academy to the Senate; the Senate had given it to the captain commander, that he might be directed by it. *De la Croyere* had also a copy of it, which he produced in the council. No land was set down upon it towards the East, but, on the contrary, there was marked on this map South-East from *Awatscha* in 46 to 47 deg. North lat. a coast extending 15 deg. from West to East, in such a manner, that it had only been seen on the South side. The words, *Terres vues par dom* Jean de Gama, [land seen by Don *Jean Gama*] were put to it. Accordingly it was judged by the maritime council, that if such a coast really existed in those parts, as they trusted the authors of the map would not have represented it on an uncertainty, then that land might extend far enough to the East, and therefore it was determined first to steer South East by East towards that land, and, having discovered it, to make its coasts serve as a guide to the North and East; but, if it should not be found in 46 deg. North lat. then to alter the coast, and to sail so long to the East, and East by North, till they should discover land, which they were to follow between North and East, or between North and West, as far as the 65th deg. North lat. and to order the voyage in such a manner as to be able to return to *Awatscha* in the month of *September*.

Since this determination is looked upon by the mariners that were in the expedition, as the source of all the misfortunes they have met with on their voyage, it is necessary to dwell a little upon the subject. It is not known who *Jean de Gama* was, nor when the discovery was made that is ascribed to him. All we know is, that, in the year 1649, *Texeira*, cosmographer to the king of *Portugal*, published a map, in which 10 or 12 deg. North East from *Japan*, in 44 to 45 deg. North

lat.

lat. is represented a multitude of islands, and a coast extending towards the East, with the following words, *Terre vue par* Jean de Gama Indien *en allant de la* Chine *à la* Nouvelle Espagne, * [land seen by *John de Gama*, the *Indian*, in going from *China* to *New-Spain*] so that the discovery has been made either at the same time as that of the ship *Castricom*, or before; and the situation of the land of *Gama*, as it is represented in *Texeira*'s maps, seems not to be distinguished from the company's land, discovered by the same ship *Castricom*. Our sailors are of opinion that they have been misled to an unprofitable navigation by *de Lisle*'s map. This is true with respect to the navigation to *America*, which, by this means, was very much retarded. But the only fault is, that M. *de Lisle* has placed the land of *Gama* too much towards the East, as belonging to the *American* discoveries, whereas it ought to have been among those of *Japan* or *Jeso*. If he had done this, the discovery of it would have been committed to Capt. *Spangberg*; and it would have been no mistake, if no more of it had been discovered than of *Jeso*, *Staten* island, or the *Company's Land*. We need not wonder if the land of *Gama*, or the *Company's Land*, have met with the same fate with the land of *Jeso*. As for the rest, it has been observed, that now the land of *Gama* is either not at all admitted by geographers, or made so minute, and placed so near *Japan*, and the *Company's Land*, that there remains hardly any difference between it and the *Company's Land*. We need but to examine in this respect the most modern maps of M. *D'Anville*, *Bellin*, *Green*, *Buache*, and even *de Lisle*'s.

Now the rest of the regulations being finished, and the ships stored with as much provisions as they could contain, the voyage was begun with both ships on the 4th of *June* 1741. They steered the course agreed upon, *viz.* South East by South, till the 12th of the said month, when they found themselves in 46 deg. North lat. There was no occasion for this to be convinced of the nullity of the lands of *Gama*. They went with a Northerly course as far as 50 deg. North lat. and intending to go from thence Easterly, in order to discover the continent of *America*, on the 20th Capt. *Tschirikow*, in a violent storm and fog, was separated from the captain commander.

This was their first misfortune, the ships were thereby deprived of the mutual assistance which they might have given each other,

* *Considerationes Geographiques et Physiques par M.* Buache, p. 128.

and

and which was the intention of fitting out two ships, and giving them instructions never to separate. The captain commander did all in his power to find *Tschirikow*; he cruized three days between 50 and 51 deg. North lat. and sailed back to the South East as far as 45 deg. but all in vain. *Tscherikow* had taken an East course, from 48 deg. North lat. which the captain commander commenced in 45 deg. so that they did not meet again; but nevertheless made discoveries which most exactly agree.

Nothing particular happened till the 18th of *July*, when the captain commander, after having given orders for steering more and more Northerly, got sight of the continent of *America* in 58 deg. 28 min. North lat. and believed, according to his journal, that he had sailed 50 deg. East long. from *Awatscha*. Capt. *Tschirikow* reached the same coast three days before, viz. on the 15th of *July* in 56 deg. North lat. and, according to his account, 60 deg. long. from *Awatscha*. But both may have been somewhat mistaken in the difference of longitude; for, if we compare their voyage thither with their return, it seems that the captain commander was on the coast of *America* in 60, and Capt. *Tschirikow* in 65 deg. long. from *Awatscha*. Now, the longitude from the harbour of *St Peter* and *Paul*, in the bay of *Awatscha*, is about 167 deg. 12 ½ min. from the first meridian of *Ferro*; consequently the longitude of the coasts of *America*, for the first place, amounts to 236, and, for the second, to 241 deg. but, if these places are considered with respect to the nearest known parts of *California*, then the difference of latitude between cape *Blanco*, the most Northerly part of *California*, and the place where Capt. *Tscherikow* was, is only 13 deg. lat. and the longitude not much above 5 deg. A distance indeed very considerable, which might deserve to be enquired into, especially as this is the place to which is ascribed the dubious discoveries of Admiral *de Fontes*. But of this our navigators had, at that time, no intelligence.

The coast made by Capt. *Tscherikow*, was steep and rocky, without any islands, wherefore he did not dare to approach it, but anchored at some distance. As he intended to enquire into the nature of the country, and, being likewise in want of fresh water, he sent the mate, *Abraham Dementiew*, with ten of his best men, and the long boat ashore, having first furnished them with provisions for some days, with guns and other arms, a brass cannon, and every other requisite, together with circumstantial instructions, how, in various occasions

occasions they ought to behave, and to make themselves understood by signals. The boat was seen to row into a bay behind a small cape. It was concluded that she was fortunately arrived ashore, because such signals were made as were ordered in that case. Several days past, but the boat did not come back; and yet signals continued without interruption. The people on board began to think the boat might have received damage in landing, and could not return to the ship without being repaired, therefore it was determined to send ashore, in the small boat, the boatswain, *Sidor Sawelew*, with three men, (another account says six men) amongst whom were carpenters, and a careener well armed and provided with the necessary materials. This was done on the 21st of *July*. *Sawelew* had orders when he had given the necessary assistance to *Dementiew* to return, either with him or by himself, to the ship. But neither of them obeyed these orders: In the mean while a great smoke was observed, arising continually from the shore.

The next day two vessels came rowing from the land towards the ship. The one was larger than the other: It was believed, on their being seen afar off, that it was *Dementiew* and *Sawelew* with the two boats. From this opinion Capt. *Tschirikow* ordered all the men upon deck, and directed them to prepare for their departure; but these were *Americans*, who, while at some distance, seeing many people upon the deck, ceased rowing, stood up, and crying out with a loud voice *Agai, Agai*, speedily returned towards the shore. If it be true, that the *Americans* were afraid of the many *Russians* on deck, and that imagining there were few or none left aboard the ship, they might therefore easily make themselves masters of it, it would then have been better for *Tschirikow* to have concealed his men. The *Americans* would, perhaps, have come on board; and, if they had, they and their vessels might have been seized, and exchanged for the *Russians* and their boats on shore. But the joy he felt at thinking that *Dementiew* and *Sawelew* were returning was so great, that no such precaution was thought of.

Now they began to give up all hopes of seeing their comrades return from shore, they had no more small boats, and durst not venture to approach the land with the ship, on account of the rocky coast; but a strong West wind arising, and the ship being at anchor towards the open sea, without shelter, they were obliged to weigh anchor, and put to sea again for fear of being driven against the rocks. *Tschirikow*

G cruized

cruized some days longer in these parts, and when the weather began to grow milder, he sailed again towards the place where his people were landed. It must be said, in his praise, that it was with regret he was obliged to leave his countrymen on such a remote coast, and among Savages; but as now he neither heard nor saw any thing of them, it was concluded, in a council of the rest of the sea officers, to return to *Kamtschatka*, which was done on the 27th of *July*.

At the time when this happened, the commander *Bering* likewise attempted to get a better account of the coast which he had discovered, and to provide himself with fresh water. The country had terrible high mountains that were covered with snow. He sailed towards it; but only small variable breezes blowing, he could reach it no sooner than the 20th of *July*, when, under a pretty large island, not far from the continent, he anchored in 22 fathoms water, and a soft clayey bottom. A point of land which there projects into the sea, they called *St Elias*'s Cape, on account of its being *Elias* day. Another headland that afterwards appeared opposite the first, towards the West, received its name from *St Hermogenes*. Between these there was a bay, in which they promised themselves security, if perhaps their circumstances should require their seeking for a harbour.

For this purpose the captain commander sent *Chitrow*, the master of the fleet, with some armed men, to reconnoitre this bay; another boat, in which was the Adjunctus *Steller*, was sent at the same time to fetch water. *Chitrow* found between some islands a convenient anchoring place, secure from all winds, but there was no occasion to make use of it. He found in an island some empty huts, and it was supposed that the inhabitants on the continent used to come thither on account of the fishery. These huts were formed of smooth boards, in some places carved; whence it may be concluded, that the inhabitants are not quite so wild and uncivilized as those in *North America* are generally described to be. In the huts he found a small box of poplar, a hollow earthen ball in which a stone rattled, like a toy for children, and a whetstone, on which it appeared that copper knives had been sharpened. So necessity teaches the making use of one metal instead of another. Even in *Siberia*, in the uppermost parts on the river *Jenisei*, all sorts of edge tools of copper have been found in the antient *Pagan* graves, and none of iron, which

(43)

is a proof that the use of copper has been of greater antiquity in those regions than that of iron.

Of *Steller*'s observations, I will only mention what is most material. He met with a cellar, and in it store of red salmon, and a sweet herb *, which is dressed for food in the same manner as in *Kamtschatka*; there lay likewise ropes, and all sorts of houshold furniture. He came to a place where the *Americans* had but just before dined, but on sight of him, were run away. There he found an arrow and a wooden instrument to procure fire, made in the same manner as they have them in *Kamtschatka* †, which things on their flight the *Americans* had left behind them. *Steller* gathered herbs, and brought such a quantity of them to the ship, that the describing of them took him up a considerable time. Of his description, *Gmelin* afterwards made use in the *Flora Siberica*. He has regretted nothing so much, as that no more time was allowed him to look about on the *American* coast. His whole stay lasted but six hours, for as soon as they had taken in fresh water, he was obliged to return on board.

The sailors, who had fetched the water, related that they had met with two fire places, where just before fire had been, and found hewn wood, and observed the steps of men in the grass; that they had seen five red foxes, which went along quite tame, being not in the least afraid of them. They brought smoaked fishes with them on board, that appeared like large carp, and tasted very well. They had found a hut thrown up of earth, which perhaps is what *Steller* called a cellar.

Having laid in a sufficient provision of water, they were willing to shew the *Americans* that they had had no reason to become fugitives from their unknown guests. Some presents were sent for them on shore; a piece of green glazed linnen, two iron kettles, two knives, twenty large beads of glass, two iron *Chinese* tobacco-pipes, and one pound of *Tscherkassian* tobacco leaves. These things were thought to be according to the taste of these people, and were carried into the above huts.

The next day, viz. the 21st of *July*, it was determined to put to sea again, it was resolved before the departure from *Awatscha*, to take

* *Sphondilium foliolis pinnatifidis.* Linn. Hort Cliff. 103.
† Namely, a board with several holes in it, and a stick, the one end of which is put into the holes, and the other turned about swiftly between the hands, till the wood within the holes begins to burn, when there is tinder ready, which catches the fire, and communicates it farther.

G 2   the

the courſe along the coaſts as far as 65 deg. N. lat. but they could get no farther to the North, and were even obliged to ſail continually more and more to the South, becauſe the coaſts extended South Weſt. At the ſame time they met with continual hindrances from the many iſlands which were very thick, almoſt every where about the continent. When they thought to ſail moſt ſecure, land was diſcovered a head, and on both ſides, wherefore they were obliged ſeveral times to turn back, and ſeek another and freer paſſage. Sometimes it came to paſs, that in the night with the ſame wind and weather, they at one time ſailed in a boiſterous ſea, and at another in calm water, and a few hours after found themſelves again between large waves, where they could hardly govern the ſhip. What elſe could this indicate, than that in the calm they had ſailed in ſheltered water, between iſlands which the darkneſs of the night did not permit them to diſcover.

Some days were paſſed without their ſeeing land, when, on the 27th of *July*, about midnight, they came into 20 fathom water. They could not know whether it was a ſand-bank, or whether they ought to take care of the continent, or of an iſland; for it was quite dark. Every where they found leſs water; to come to an anchor they durſt not venture, for the wind was ſtrong, an i the waves high. Moreover it was to be feared that they might be either too far from the ſhore, or too near it. At laſt it was concluded to hazard ſailing to the South, in which they ſucceeded ſo well, that, after ſteering ſome hours longer in 20 fathoms water, they regained a ſecure ſea.

An iſland, which they diſcovered on the 30th of *July*, in foggy weather, was called *Tumannoi Oſtrog*, that is, the *Foggy Iſland*. They arrived at it in 7 or 8 fathoms water, and anchored with great expedition. But when it began to clear up, they found themſelves a Werſt from it. The whole month of *Auguſt* elapſed with the like occurrences; when the ſhip's crew begun to be much affected with the ſcurvey, and particularly the captain commander.

When their freſh water began to be reduced to a ſmall quantity, they ran, on the 29th of *Auguſt*, to the North, and immediately again diſcovered the continent, and before it a multitude of iſlands, between which they anchored. Theſe iſlands are ſituated in 55 deg. 25 min. N. lat. They were called the *Schumagins* iſlands, after the name of the firſt of the ſhip's company, who died in the voyage, and was buried here. On the 30th of *Auguſt*, the pilot *Andrew Heſſelberg* was ſent to one of the largeſt iſlands, in ſearch of freſh water. He

did

did not stay long, and brought two samples of water, which, although they were not found to be very good, they being of a brackish taste, yet, as there was no time to lose, they thought it was better to have this water than none at all, as it might at least serve for boiling, while what they had still left being used sparingly might hold out for drinking. *Steller* afterwards attributed to this water the scurvy and other distempers which prevailed among the sailors.

The ship lay not very secure, she was exposed to all the Southerly winds, and to the North they had nothing but rocks and cliffs before them; wherefore they would not venture to be long at anchor in this place; but as, in the night before, a fire had been seen on a small island towards the N. N. E. while they fetched water with the yawls, they sent *Chitrow* in the small boat, with five men, among whom was a *Tschucktschian* interpreter; they were all well armed, and had some trifles given them to distribute among the people they should find. On the 30th of *August*, about noon, they arrived on the island; which was computed about six leagues distance from the ship; there was yet fires to be seen, but the people were gone. In the afternoon *Chitrow* intended to return to the ship, but a strong contrary wind drove them on another island, and detained them till the 2d of *September*, when the storm ceased. *Chitrow* not returning the same day, the large boat was sent for him next morning, the small boat had received too much hurt, when she was thrown on shore by the waves for them to venture with her to sea again; she was therefore left on the island, and *Chitrow* returned on board in the large boat.

Immediately dispositions were made to weigh anchor, and put to sea again; but they could not advance much, because of the strong contrary winds, but were forced towards the evening to seek again a place of security, between the islands. On the 4th of *September* it was the same; they set sail, but the continual vehement contrary wind forced them back to their former anchoring place; during the night there was a violent storm.

The next morning they heard on one of the islands a loud cry of men, and observed fire burning. Soon after two *Americans* came rowing towards the ship, in two canoes, shaped like those used by the savages in *Greenland*, and *Davis*'s streights, but they stopped at some distance. The calumets used by the *North American* nations to express their peaceable sentiments were known; and these people were

observed

observed to have them; they were sticks with hawks wings tied to one end. The people seemed as well by words, as gestures, to invite our mariners on shore; as, on the other hand, these latter by beckoning and throwing presents to them to bring them to the ship; but the *Americans* would not be persuaded, but turned back to their island.

It was resolved to pay them a visit on shore, lieutenant *Waxel*, accompanied by nine men, all well provided with arms, went to the island. Our people tried first to invite the *Americans*, nine of whom stood on the shore, to them in the boat, by a friendly behaviour, and offering of various presents; but as this proved fruitless, and the *Americans*, on their part, invited the *Russians* to them on shore; *Waxel* ordered three men of his company to debark, among whom was a *Tschuktschian*, or *Korjak* interpreter, and to fasten the boat with a rope to the stones, at some distance from the shore. It has been observed every where that the *Tschuktschian*, and *Korjak* interpreters, did not understand the language of these people; but they were nevertheless very serviceable, as conductors, being bold, and looked upon by the *Americans*, as the same with themselves. The whole conversation consequently consisted here merely in gestures and signs, by which on both sides they shewed great good will. The *Americans* had a mind to regale the *Russians*, and gave them whale's flesh, as the only provision they had. It seems they were there only on account of the whale fishery; for our people observed, on the shore, as many canoes as there were men, but neither huts nor women; from whence 'tis to be concluded, that their habitations were on the continent.

The canoes were shaped like those that had been seen before, not larger than to hold one man. In the middle there is a round opening, in which the *American* seats himself, and ties the leather so fast to his body, that not a drop of water can penetrate into the canoe.

No bows and arrows, nor any other weapon, were seen among these *Americans*, of which our *Russians* might have been afraid, and therefore they stayed pretty long on shore, and went about with the *Americans*, yet so that they did not lose sight of the boats as they were ordered.

In the mean while, one of the *Americans* had the courage to come to lieutenant *Waxel* in the boat, he seemed to be the oldest and most important. *Waxel* presented to him a cup of brandy, but this was a quite unknown and disagreeable liquor to him; he spit the brandy out again,

again, as foon as he had tafted it, and cried aloud, as if he was complaining to his country men how ill he was ufed. He would by no means be appeafed; needles, glafs beads, an iron kettle, tobacco-pipes, &c. were offered him, but he accepted of nothing; he only defired to return to the ifland, and it was not thought proper to detain him. *Waxel*, on his part alfo, called to his people that were on fhore, to come back.

This the *Americans* did not like; they made an attempt to keep all three with them. At laft they let go the two *Ruffians*, and kept the interpreter. Some of them went to lay hold of the rope with which the fhip's boat was faftened to the fhore, they pulled as hard as they could, probably thinking that it was as eafily to be drawn on fhore as their fmall canoes. To prevent which, *Waxel* ordered the rope to be cut. The interpreter called out to them not to abandon him; the talking and beckoning out of the boat to the *Americans* to defift from him, was to no purpofe; wherefore *Waxel* difcharged two blunderbuffes, which, as it was merely done with a defign to frighten them, had the defire effect. The unufual noife of the report, which was increafed by the echo from a neighbouring mountain, threw all the *Americans* ftunned to the ground, and the interpreter efcaped out of their hands; foon after they recovered themfelves, they fhewed themfelves very angry by their geftures and noife, and indicated that no body fhould come to them on fhore. The night now approached, it was ftormy weather, and the fhip lay two Werfts diftance; wherefore *Waxel* did not think it advifeable to try thefe people further.

I have faid before, that no bows and arrows were obferved among the *Americans*, but this does not prove that they ufe none, but confirms the opinion only that at this time they were out on the whale fifhery, for which purpofe fuch arms are not ufed. One fingle man had a knife hanging by his fide, of which, on account of its particular make, our people feemed to take notice; the defign of it cannot be conjectured. Their upper garment was made of whales guts, their breeches of feal-fkins, and their caps of the fkins of fea lions, which in *Kamtfchatka* are called *frwutfcha*, and adorned with various feathers, efpecially thofe of hawk's. They had their nofes ftopt with grafs, which fometimes they took out, when a great deal of matter iffued out, which they licked up with their tongues; their faces were painted red, and fome of various colours, and differently fhaped like thofe of the *Europeans*; fome had flat nofes as the *Calmucks*, and all

were

were of pretty good stature. It is probable that they chiefly feed on the sea animals, which are caught in those seas. These are the whales, the sea lions, and bears, the sea beaver, or rather sea-otters, and seals.

They were observed to eat roots too, which they sought out of the ground, and before they eat them scarce shaked off the earth. What might be farther added here is only this, that a certain person maintains that he made himself understood, in some measure by these people by the list of words, which *La Hontan* has subjoined to his description of *North America*. For having pronounced according to the said list, the words *water*, or *wood*, the people had pointed to such parts where these things are found; but, I think, this they may have done by chance, or the gestures, which accompanied the words, may have contributed to render them intelligible; for *La Hontan* is not to be placed among the conscientious and credible writers of travels. But, setting aside this, the distance between the countries is two great for one and the same language to be spoken in them; not to maintain, that an *European*, particularly a *Frenchman*, will hardly conceive and write the words of such a language in such a manner as to be intelligible to another nation, that speaks nearly the same language.

Lieut. *Waxel* returned to the ship, and the next morning prepared for his departure, when seven of the *Americans*, whom he had left the day before, arrived in so many canoes, in which they approached near the vessel. Two of them rose up in the canoes, laid hold of the rope ladders of the ship, and delivered as presents two of their caps, and the image of a man carved out of bone, which was taken for an idol. The usual mark of peace the Calumet was again offered; it consisted of a stick five feet long; to the upper and inner part of which were tied many sorts of feathers without the least order. Whence we see that the similitude of the Calumet to *Mercury*'s staff, as the *American* travellers represent it, is not essentially necessary. Presents were reciprocally made, and they would certainly have come aboard, if the wind had not begun to rise, and obliged them to return to the shore with all expedition. After their having returned to land, they assembled in a cluster, and made a great noise, which lasted almost a quarter of an hour. Soon after our people set sail, and when they passed the island on which the *Americans* were, these again began to make as great a noise as ever they could, which may as well be taken for a token of friendship, whereby they intended to express their wishing them a happy voyage, as their rejoicing at getting rid of their strange guests

guests. They steered for the most part southerly, to get clear of the coast, and indeed could keep no other course, the wind blowing W. and W. S. W. From this time till late in Autumn, when the voyage was finished, the wind seldom changed, but between W. S. W. and W. N. W. so that there is reason to believe, that, at this time of the year, the westerly winds blow almost continually in those parts. When an easterly gale sometimes arose, it did not last above a few hours, and then shifted westerly again. This was a great hindrance in their return; besides the weather was continually so foggy, that sometimes for two or three weeks together the sun could neither be seen by day, nor the stars by night, and therefore no observations of the latitude could be made, and, consequently, the ship's reckoning could not be corrected. What inquietude this must have caused in our navigators, who were thus steering in an unknown sea, with long uncertainty, is scarce to be conceived. An officer, who was with them, has expressed himself on this subject, in his relation of this voyage, in the following manner. "I do not know whether " there can be a more discontented and worse manner of living in the " world, than to navigate an undescribed sea. I speak from experi- " ence, and can say with truth, that during the five months I was in " this voyage, without seeing any land known before, I did not sleep " quietly many hours; because I was in continual danger and uncer- " tainty."

They had mostly contrary winds and storms, till the 24th of *September*, when they saw land again, which consisted of very high mountains, and many islands were lying before them at a great distance. Here they computed that they were in 51 deg. 27 min. N. lat. and 21 deg. 39 min. long. from the harbour of St *Peter* and *Paul* at *Awatscha*. As it was the day of the Conception of St *John* the Baptist, one of the highest mountains on the coast was named St *John*'s mountain. Afterwards to determine the situation of the coast more exactly, it was supposed to be in the latitude of 52 deg. 30 min. which, however, is contradicted by Capt. *Tschirikow*'s account, who had also been on this coast, and placed it in 51 deg. 12 min. as is mentioned hereafter.

Nothing farther happened here, since they durst not approach the coast, on account of a strong south wind; but, it was thought adviseable to tack about against the wind, which soon after changed to a violent storm from the west, and drove the ship very far towards

H   the

the S. E. The storm continued without interruption for 17 days, of which we can find but few instances, for the pilot *Andrew Hesselberg*, a man who had been in the sea service 50 years, in several parts of the world, owned that he had never seen such a long continued storm in his life. They in the mean while, carried as few sails as they could, without being driven too far; but how far they were driven back may, in some measure, be concluded by their finding themselves, on the 12th of *October*, when the storm abated, in 48 deg. 18 min. N. lat. This is to be understood according to the ship's reckoning; for the continual dark weather would not permit their making observations.

Many of the ship's crew had before been taken sick, but now the scurvy began to break out more and more; seldom a day passed without some of them dying, and scarce so many retained their health as were necessary to govern the ship.

In these circumstances it was difficult to determine, whether they should endeavour to return to *Kamtschatka*, or seek a harbour some where on the *American* coast. This latter the general calamity, (the late season, the want of fresh water, and the very great distance from the harbour of St. *Peter* and *Paul*) seemed to require, but in a council of the officers, the first was resolved upon, and the wind springing up favourable, they again sailed North, and from the 15th of *October* towards the West. They passed by an island, which they ought to have seen in their going out, according to the course of the ship, as described in the map, nay *Steller* has mentioned, in one account, that in going out land had been seen in these parts, but the ship's journals contain nothing of it, and it is difficult to believe, that they would have sought so far for the land, had they found it before much nearer. The mistake may rather have happened in describing the course on the map, an error, which, in an unknown sea, may easily have creped in, or the island, in going out, might be concealed by a fog. This island was called after *St. Macarius*, so the others that followed in the west obtained the names of St. *Stephen*, St. *Theodore*, and St. *Abraham*.

On the 29th and 30th of *October*, they approached two islands which they left without names, as according to their situation, size, and other exterior appearances, they resembled the two first *Kurilian* islands, for which they were taken, and therefore they bent their
course

course to the north, but had they continued to steer to the west only two days longer, they would have made the harbour of *Awatscha*. I therefore call these islands the [*Isles de la Seduction*] *Seducing Islands*, but the seduction which they occasioned was of the worst consequence.

When the long wished for coast of *Kamtschatka* did not appear towards the west, they then had no hopes of a harbour, and the men, notwithstanding their want, misery, and sickness, were obliged to work continually in the cold and wet, which made every one despair; and the sickness was so dreadful that the two sailors, who used to be at the rudder, were obliged to be led to it by two others who could hardly walk And when one could set and steer no longer, another in little better condition, supplied his place. Many sails they durst not hoist, because there was nobody to lower them in case of need, and indeed they were so thin and rotten that a violent wind would have torn them to pieces, and they were not in a condition to make others for want of hands.

The continual rains now began to change into hail and snow; the nights grew longer and darker, they knew not in what latitude they were, or how far from *Kamtschatka*. How glad were they when the next morning at 8 o'clock land appeared.

They endeavour'd to approach it, but it was yet at a great distance: For, in the beginning, they only discerned the tops of the mountains, that were covered with snow, and when they might have reached it, the night began to come on, during which it was more advisable to keep the sea, that they might not expose the ship to danger.

The next morning they saw that most of the ropes on the starboard side of the ship were broken; nothing more was wanting to complete their misfortune; for, as almost all the people were sick, none were able to remedy this evil.

Lieut, *Waxel* who gave intelligence of it to the captain commander, received orders to call together all the officers, to consult what was to be done. This council was held, and the danger where with all were threatened, the ship being rendered unfit for farther navigation, on account of her poor tackle was taken in consideration. The want of water, and the sicknesses increased; and, as the continual wet, had caused a great inconvenience hitherto, they became the more sensible of the cold now, as the late season promised no mitigations, but rather threatened an increase of it. All this considered, the result was, that they should sail towards the discovered land, and endeavour, at least, to save their lives; perhaps the ship might likewise be brought in; but, if this could not be done, then they must commit their farther fate to providence.

Immediately they steered towards the land; the wind was northerly, and they sailed W. S. W. and S. W. They sounded, and found by the lead 37 fathoms water, and a sandy ground. At five o'clock in the evening, they were, by the lead, in 12 fathoms water, having the same ground. Here they cast out one anchor, with 3 quarters of the cable, which, at 6 o'clock, tore in pieces. Vast waves drove the ship on a rock, which she touched twice, notwithstanding, by the lead, they found five fathoms water; at the same time the waves rolled over the ship several times, with such vehemence that it made her shake; they droped the second anchor, the cable of which was tore in pieces before they observed that the anchor had taken ground.

A high sea threw the vessel on the other side of the rock, when they were just about getting ready another anchor. All at once they got into still water, and anchored in a depth of four fathoms, and a half in sandy ground, about 300 fathoms from the shore.

As they were obliged to take up their winter quarters here, the first care was to look about on shore, and choose the most convenient place for it. The ship's company quite weak, having rested a little till noon, they brought the boat over board not with out a great deal of trouble. On the 6th of *November*, at one o'clock, Lieutenant *Waxel*, and Adjunctus *Steller* went on shore, which was quite covered with snow. A brook running from the mountains, and falling into the sea, not far from the landing place, was not yet frozen, and consisted of clear wholesome water; but no forests were seen, nay not so much as fire-wood, except what was thrown on shore by the sea, and even that was already covered with snow, and not easily to be found. They could neither build houses or barracks, nor shelter their sick; or knew they how to defend themselves against the cold; But necessity the mother of invention, pointed out near the brook just mentioned many sandy hills, and between them pretty deep ditches; these they resolved to clear somewhat below, and cover them with sails, in order to dwell in them, at least till they should be provided with wood thrown on shore sufficient to build huts, however indifferent they might be. Towards the evening

Waxel

Waxel and *Steller* returned to the ſhip, and gave an account to the Captain Commander of what they had ſeen.

It was concluded to ſend on ſhore the next morning as many men as were yet able to ſtand on their legs, to prepare firſt of all as conveniently as poſſible a ditch between the ſaid hills, for the reception of the ſick. The 8th of *November*, a beginning was made to land the ſick, but ſome died as ſoon as they were brought from between decks, in the open air, others during the time they were on the deck, ſome in the boat, and many more as ſoon as they were brought on ſhore.

The ſtone foxes, of which a great many harboured in this place, were obſerved to fall very eagerly upon the corpſe. It was thought that they had never been ſcared by men, except thoſe that now for the firſt time ſet foot on this land; and, therefore, they were not in the leaſt afraid of them, and did not run away when any body approached them. It required ſome trouble to keep them from the dead bodies; this circumſtance gave occaſion already to ſuppoſe this to be an iſland, as it proved.

On the 9th of *November*, the Captain Commander, *Bering*, was brought on ſhore, being carried by four men on a hand barrow, which conſiſted of two poles, bound round with ropes, and well ſecured from the open air. Every day they continued bringing on ſhore the ſick; and daily ſome of them died. None of thoſe, who on board were confined to their beds, recovered; who were chiefly ſuch as by indifference and faint heartedneſs had much contributed to the increaſe of the ſickneſs.

This diſtemper begins with a weakneſs over the whole body, and renders the patient heavy and averſe to all buſineſs, caſts the mind quite down, and by degrees cauſes a ſhortneſs of breath from the leaſt exerciſe; ſo thoſe affected with it chooſe rather to lay down than to walk; but this is the patient's deſtruction; for it is followed by a pain in all the limbs, the feet begin to ſwell, the face grows quite yellow, and the body is covered with blue ſpots, the mouth and the gums bleed, and all the teeth grow looſe, then the patient commonly does not care to ſtir, but becomes quite indifferent with regard to life or death. Theſe ſeveral degrees of the ſickneſs, and their effects were gradually ſeen on board the ſhip. Some of the patients were obſerved to be ſubject to a fearful anxiety, and that any noiſe (which on board of a ſhip is unavoidable) put them in a fright; notwithſtanding which many eat their victuals with a good appetite, not thinking them-so ill as in reality they were. For when orders were given to land the sick, they very chearfully put on their cloaths, and believed they should now be speedily cured; but, as soon as they got from their couch, which was in a lower part of the vessel, upon deck, and in the open air, they died.

Those alone were best of, that did not suffer themselves to be conquered by the distemper so far as to keep their bed constantly, but strove to remain on their legs, and in exercise, as much as possible, and whose lively disposition prevented them from despair. Such among them were of great service to the other, as well by their example as persuasion. This has been observed in particular among the officers, who, being continually employed in affairs relating to the command, and to take care that nothing might be neglected, were obliged to spend most of their time upon the deck. They had always a great deal of exercise.

But with the Captain Commander all this was to no purpose; his age, and the disposition of his body, were the cause of his being inclined more for rest than for exercise. He grew at last diffident, and looked upon every one as his enemy, insomuch, that even he could not bear the sight of *Steller*, for whom before he had so great an affection.

Waxel and *Chitrow* remained tolerably healthy as long as they were at sea; they continued longest on board, not only because they would see every thing brought on shore, but because they also had more conveniency in the ship. But in a few days they also grew so sick, that, on the 21st of *November*, they were carried on shore like the rest. Experience having taught how to behave in going out of the ship, and in entering in the free air; the patients were carefully wrapt up, and not suffered to partake of the open air, by a free transpiration, till by degrees they had been used to it. Afterwards both were restored to health.

The Captain Commander, *Bering*, died on the 8th of *December*, and had the honour to have the island called *Bering*'s island, after his name. He was a *Dane* by birth, and had, in his youth, made voyages to the *East* and *West Indies*, when the glorious example of the immortal emperor *Peter* the Great for the marine tempted him to seek his fortune in *Russia*. I have found it some where, that, in the year 1707, he was lieutenant, and, in 1710, captain lieutenant in the

Russian

Ruffian fleet. When he was made a Captain I cannot exactly determine. Having thus served in the *Cronstadt* fleet from its beginning; and been in all the expeditions by sea, in the war with the *Swedes*, he joined to the capacity requisite for his office, a long experience, which made him particularly worthy of such extraordinary exploits, as were the discoveries wherewith he had been twice intrusted. It is a pity that it was his fate to end his life in such an unfortunate manner. He may be said to have been buried half alive, for the sand rolling down continually from the side of the ditch in which he lay, and covering his feet, he at last would not suffer it to be removed, and said, that he felt some warmth from it, which otherwise he should want in the remaining parts of his body, and thus the sand increased to his belly; so that after his decease they were obliged to scrape him out of the ground, in order to inter him in a proper manner.

On the 27th of *July*, Captain *Tschirikow* sailed on his return from the *American* coast, and suffered almost the same accidents as the Captain Commander. Meeting with contrary winds, and other impediments from the coasts and islands, the not discovery of which on their going out they greatly lamented. Nay, he had one still greater inconveniency than the former, *viz.* that on account of the loss of his two boats he could not provide himself with fresh water.

On the 20th of *September* he arrived in 51 deg. 12 min. north lat. on a coast, which they suppose to have been the same that four days after the Captain Commander also arrived at. This coast was surrounded with rocks, the tops of which reached above the water, so that they were obliged to take all imaginable pains to escape a danger that, on a nearer approach, would have been unavoidable. They found themselves obliged to anchor at 200 fathoms distance from it. Twenty-one of the inhabitants of the country came rowing, every one in his leather canoe, with a friendly mien, as if they intended to assist our people, and full of astonishment about the ship, which they could not behold enough. But no body could speak with them; neither durst our ship tarry, because the cable was torn to pieces by the rocks, and the crew were forced to endeavour to regain the open sea, which although they succeeded, it was but of little advantage to the passage, because of the contrary winds.

The fresh water beginning to decrease, they thought to help themselves, by distilling the sea water; and indeed they did thereby deprive

prive it of its salt, but the bitterness remained. In the mean time nothing else was to be done than to mix the distilled sea water with an equal part of the remaining fresh water, which they distributed in small portions, to make it go the farther. What joy was there when in this distress it rained! For then they refreshed themselves with the rain water that they had gathered, and its being pressed out of the sails gave them no aversion to it.

One may easily conceive that this circumstance must increase the scurvy, on board of *Tschirickow's* ship whereby many were swept away. The captain himself lay continually sick from the 20th of *September*. At last on the 8th of *October*, they came in sight of the land of *Kamtschatka*, and on the 9th they entered the bay of *Awatscha*. On the 10th *De la Croyere*, who had been lingering too for a long while, wanted to go on shore, but when he came upon deck, he fell down dead. Of 70 men, which was the whole number of the ship's company, they counted 21 dead. The pilot *Jelagin*, who was the only officer, that had his health yet, brought the ship back into the harbour of St *Peter* and *Paul* on the 11th, after she had spent in this voyage above four months.

In the following spring Captain *Tschirikow*, who, in the mean time, was recovered from his sickness, cruzed about in the sea, in hopes of meeting with the Captain Commander, then sailed to *Ochotzk*, from whence he travelled to *Jakutzk*, where he expected orders from *Petersburg* what was farther to be done. He was obliged to make some stay at *Jeseisk*. On his return, at *Petersburg* he was appointed Captain Commander; but died soon after.

But let us return to the *Bering's* island; where, a little before the death of the captain, the company had the misfortune to lose their chief comfort and hopes, the only means by which, in their opinion, they could be delivered out of their distress, I mean the vessel. She rode at anchor, as we have seen already, towards the open sea; not a soul was left on board to guard her, as the few people that were yet on their legs, were wanted for attending the sick and other business. A violent storm arsing from E. S. E. in the night between the 28th and 29th of *November*, the cable was tore to pieces, and the ship drove on shore, not far from the place where our people lay in the ditches, and settled in the sand from 8 to 9 feet, the bottom and sides must at the same time have been very much damaged; For it was observed, that with the flood the sea water penetrated into her from below,

to

and with the ebb ran out again. By this mean most of their meal, and salt was lost, as the chief of their provisions were on board; and, although at low water a good deal was saved, yet it had suffered much damage; it was very fortunate that the ship was cast on shore, and not driven into the sea. For, in the last case, these poor people must have been obliged to abide, as long as they lived, on this desert island, where no wood grows, of which they might have built another vessel. But there were now hopes left, that, though the ship itself could not be refitted for service, they might build a vessel for their return to *Kamtschatka*. They now therefore submitted to their fate, and only endeavoured to prolong their lives as much as possible; for which purpose the following dispositions were made.

In the first place, it was necessary to search the country in order to discover whether it was a continent or island; for of this they could not be certain in the beginning. Rocky mountains were seen, which seemed to indicate the first; and, indeed, this island may have been formerly a part of the continent, though perhaps separated from it by earthquakes. They wanted to know, whether any inhabitants were to be found, of whom they could get assistance. It was of importance to learn, whether any forest could be discovered, and what animals and other productions of nature the country yielded. People were sent out towards the north and south, who went as far as the high rocks projecting into the sea would permit them. Some returned in two, others in three days. Their unanimous account was, that they had no where found so much as the vestiges of men. But they had every where along the coast met with many sea-beavers, *viz.* such as in *Kamtschatka* are called beavers, but ought properly to be called sea-otters *; and farther in the country they had seen a multitude of stone-foxes, both blue and white ones, which were not in the least shy of men; from whence they concluded, that these animals had never seen any men before them. After this, others were sent into the country: these went about 12 or 13 wersts from the shore, and, on a high mountain, discerned, towards the west, the open sea, in the same manner as it appeared towards the east. Now they were convinced that they were on an island. They could see no forests, and the floating wood found during the winter, was scarce sufficient for firing; for they were obliged to seek

* *Lutra marina Margravii, Brasiliensium Jaga f. Cariguibeiu.*

I

it from under the snow; but, as the snow melted, there was no farther want of it, which was a proof that on some neighbouring land there must be forrests from whence the wood came floating.

The largest breadth of the island was computed to be above twenty odd werfts, but its length, extending from south-east to north-west, has not been exactly determined. It lies in the same direction with the mouth of the river *Kamtschatka*, and the distance between both, was reckoned, in the following voyage, to be thirty *German* miles, or sixty leagues. There are many high mountains and rocks; in the valleys between which there is, in the meadows, good fresh water and high grass. On the banks of the brooks there grew low bushes of willows, but they are of no use, as the branches are not above the thickness of a finger. Pains were taken to see whether a place could be found where a ship might ride secure from winds; but they could discover none. The flood rises from seven to eight feet. Of land-animals, none have been observed, except the above-mentioned stone-foxes, and of them more blue than white ones; but their hair was not so soft as of those in *Siberia*, which may perhaps be owing to the difference of the food and air.

It was resolved to examine what store of provisions there was, and compute how long they would last, to regulate the distribution of the shares accordingly, notwithstanding which 30 persons died on the island. They found the stores were so much exhausted that if they had not been supplied with the flesh of sea-animals they must have all perished for want of food. Eight hundred pounds of meal were kept in reserve to be used in the next voyage, in case they should be so happy as to construct another vessel, in which they might return to *Kamtschatka*. Here was no respect of persons; officers and men had the same portions, and so they messed together, though in seperate companies, throughout the several ditches in which they dwelled. The state of natural liberty and equality of men, seemed here to be restored, and therefore properly no command, according to the prescribed rules, could have place. For, although, after the decease of the captain commander, Lieut. *Waxel* took the command upon himself, yet he did not chuse to correct any for fear that they would be revenged on him in private.

As to the sea-animals that served them for food, they had none at first but the above-said beavers, the meat whereof, especially that of the males, was found insipid, hard, and as tough as leather;

so that they were obliged to cut it in small pieces before they could chew it. One of these beavers may contain from forty to fifty pounds solid flesh. The entrails and guts were mostly used as food by the sick. *Steller* has exactly described some of these sea-animals; which description is inserted in the commentaries of the Academy of Sciences. In it he prescribes the flesh of the beavers as a remedy against the scurvy. A great multitude of beavers were killed, when even their flesh was no longer used for meat, only on account of their fine skins, for every one of which the *Chinese* on the frontiers at *Kjachta* pay from 80 to 100 rubles. This was still a comfort for our ship's-company. They amassed near 900 of these skins, which were divided among them all; but here none had better luck than *Steller*, for being physician, many skins were given him as presents, and others he bought of those, who, in an uncertainty, whether ever they should meet again with men, among whom they might be of use to them, did not value these goods. His share only is said to have amounted to 300 beaver-skins, which he brought with him to *Kamtschatka* and *Siberia*.

It also happened, in the beginning of the winter, that a dead whale from the sea was thrown on the island, which occasioned great joy among our people, though they were obliged to go five wersts after it. It was about eight fathoms long, and might perhaps have floated a pretty while in the sea, for the fat was already somewhat sourish; but this did not hinder our people from making use of it. They called the whale their magazine of provision, because it was a certain resource in case they should be in want of other animals. The fat was cut in small square pieces, and boiled a long time in water, to extract from it the most fluid parts, and the remaining hard and sinewy parts were swallowed unchewed, like the flesh. Afterwards, in the spring, the sea threw on shore another whale, which was much fresher than the former, and they dressed it in the same manner.

The beavers disappeared in the month of *March*, and instead of them another animal appeared, called in *Kamtschatka* a sea-cat, on account of its long hairs standing out on both sides of the mouth, as those of the cats. *Dampier* who has described it, met with many of them in his voyage on the South Sea, and gives it the name of the sea-bear. The western shore of the island was as if it were covered by them

them. These animals keep together in a family-like manner, so that a male, which has generally from 15 to 20 females, keeps them and his children so long with him, as well by sea as by land, till they begin their own house-keeping. The largest weigh from 18 to 20 pouds, that is towards 800 pounds. It is a very savage animal, inclinable to fighting, and difficult to come at; but they killed no more of these than was absolutely necessary, for the flesh has a very loathsome rank taste, and the skin is hardly good for any thing at all, except that of quite young ones, and those taken out of the womb, which are, in some measure, useful as furs. They were mostly killed a-sleep, for the old ones, in the spring time, (spend a couple of months in sleeping, without taking the least food, as the fat bears do in the depth of winter.

When these disappeared, it was near the end of the month of *May*, then the ship's crew had for some time no other sustenance than the large seals, which, in *Kamtschatka*, are called *Lachtak*. They are as big as an ox, weighing about 800 pounds a piece, but the flesh being of a loathsome taste, it was lucky that sometimes they could catch sea-lions, which afforded them better food.

The sea-lion is the animal, which, in *Kamtschatka*, is called *Scivutscha*. They are as big again as the largest sea-bears, and weigh from 36 to 40 pouds, that is about 1600 pounds; they are distinguished from the rest of the sea-animals by their short and yellow hair. As these pursue the sea-bears, it may be the reason that the latter betake themselves so abundantly to the coasts; whither the sea-lions seldom resort. They mostly post themselves at some distance from the shore, on large stones and rocks in the sea, that, to appearance, have been separated from the continent by earthquakes. Here these animals make such a terrible roaring, that they may be heard at three or four wersts distance. All other beasts flee as soon as the sea-lion appears. Their fierce and grim look bespeak their ferocity: Wherefore our ship's crew unwillingly attacked them. They only killed a few old ones a-sleep, but several of the young ones, the flesh of which was found particularly favoury. *Dampier* described them before *Steller*. Their similitude to the lion consists merely in long hair standing up, which grows about the neck of the male.

They also lived sometimes upon the flesh of the animals, which, in the *Russian* language, as well as in the *Dutch* and *English*, is called
the

the sea-cow; the *Spaniards* name it *Manati*, and the *French Lamentin*. One would think its similitude with a cow must be very great, as it appeared so to different nations and travellers at first sight, when people are used to give names to things that were unknown to them before. But this likeness consists in nothing else than the snout, which, probably, they saw first, and perhaps alone: for it has neither horns nor straight ears, no feet, nor any thing else resembling a cow. It is an animal like a seal, only incomparably larger; has two fins on the fore part of the body, wherewith it swims; between them are seen two teats in the females, for suckling its young ones. This disposition of parts being somewhat similar with the human, especially since the mother makes use of the fins to hold her young ones close to the teats, is the reason for the *Spanish* name *Manati*, i. e. *the handed animal*; for the *Spaniards* compared the fins to the hands of men. *Lamentin* it was first called by the *French*, because it does not cry loud, but in a manner whines and sighs. *Christopher Columbus* is said to have taken it for the Syren of the ancients. When it swims in the sea, one part of its back stands commonly out of the water, which is said to appear like a boat overset floating on the sea. It is not only found in these seas, but in all others surrounding *Asia*, *Africa*, and *America*, wherefore many travellers, for instance, *Lopez*, *Dampier*, *Kolb*, *Atkins*, and *Labat*, have made mention of it, but they contradict one another too frequently, which also has occasioned many mistakes in the natural history of *Clusius*, *Johnston*, *Rajus*, *Klein*, *Artedi*, *Linnæus*, and others, for the rectifying of all which, *Steller*'s description is hardly sufficient. A particular species of these animals harbours in the river *Amazon* in *South America*, and an account of it is given by M. *de la Condamine* in his travels.

I return to my design, to shew how useful the *Manati* was to our ship's company with respect to their sustenance. Some of these animals have been caught, which from the snout to the point of the tail were from three to four fathoms long, and weighed 200 pouds, or 8000 pounds. One was food enough to serve for a fortnight, and the flesh was very savoury like the best beef; that of the young ones, was like veal. And the sick found themselves considerably better, when, instead of the disagreeable hard beaver's flesh, they eat of the Manati, tho' it cost them more trouble to catch than one of the beavers. They never came on the land, but only approached the coast to eat sea-grafs, which grows on the shore, or is thrown out by the sea.

This

This good food may, perhaps, contribute a great deal to give the flesh a more disagreeable taste than that of the other animals that live on fish. The young ones that weighed 1200 pounds and upwards, remained sometimes at low water on the dry land between the rocks, which afforded a fine opportunity for killing them; but the old ones which were more cautious, and went off at the right time with the ebb, could be caught no otherwise than with harpoons, fixed to long ropes. Sometimes the ropes were broke, and the animal escaped before it could be struck a second time. This animal was seen as well in the winter as in the summer time. They melted some of the fat, with which, like hogs, they are covered from three to four inches thick, and used it as butter. Of the flesh, several casks full were pickled for ship's provision, which did excellent service on their return.

The month of *March* 1742, being near concluded, and the ground becoming free from snow, Lieut. *Waxel* called together the remainder of the ship's company, being 45, to consult with them, and to come to a resolution in what manner it was best to return. Here the meanest of the sailors had the same right to give his vote as the commanding officer: After they had all given their various opinions, *Waxel* and *Chitrow* made the proposal to break up the packet-boat, and to build a less vessel of the wood, which would contain all the company, with sufficient provisions for a fortnight, by which means those who had been fellow-sufferers might equally partake of the deliverance out of their distress. If a new misfortune was to happen, they should remain together, and there would be no reproaching of one another. This was unanimously agreed to, and a writing drawn up, which every one confirmed by signing his name to it. But, notwithstanding, there was opposition enough afterwards; some refused to break up a ship which had been built at the expence of the crown: But the contumacious were obliged to yield, being outvoted in a new council. In the beginning of the month of *April* they began to untackle and take to pieces the wreck; a work which lasted the whole month, and at which the officers were always the most assiduous, in order to encourage, by their example, the common men to imitate them.

The greatest difficulty was, who should have the direction of building of the vessel. For they wanted a ship's carpenter, three of them that set out on the voyage, died in the island. Luckily a *Siberian Cossack*, named *Sawa Starodubzow*, a native of *Krasnojarsk*,

who

(63)

who had been employed as a workman in building of ships at O-*chotzk*, offered to take upon him the management of the work, if they would but give him his proportion of the vessel. Indeed the *Cossack* kept his word as well as could be wished; and, after his return, had the favour bestowed upon him, for his services, to be made a *Sinbojarskoi*, by the provincial chancery of *Jeniseisk*, which is the lowest degree of the *Siberian* nobility. On the 6th of *May* the vessel was put on the stocks, 40 feet long in the keel, 13 feet broad, and six feet and half deep. At the end of the month, all the timbers were set in, so that in the beginning of *June* they could begin to plank her as well within as without. A deck was made, and the vessel provided with a mast, and eight oars. There was no want of hemp and old tow for careening, but the quantity of tar not being sufficient, they helped themselves in the following manner: They took a new cable, which never had been in the water, chopped it to pieces, each piece a foot long, then pulled the threads asunder, and filled a large copper kettle with them, to which they made a tight cover with a hole in the middle. Then they took a wooden vessel, which had a cover made in the same manner as the former, with a hole in the middle, this was stuck into the ground as far as the cover, they set the copper kettle upon it upside down, so that one cover and one hole hit the other. Then so much earth was laid about the kettle, that no fire could penetrate to the wooden vessel. After which fire was laid round about the kettle, the lower part of which did now stand up, more than half above the earth. From the heat, the tar, contained in the tow melted, and gathered in the wooden vessel below. By this means they got so much tar as was requisite to tar the lower part of the vessel. Her upper part was payd over with melted tallow. In the same manner they built a canoe, which would hold from eight to ten men; while all this was executing, masts and sails, ropes and anchors, water-casks, and sea provisions were procured, and every thing put in proper order.

At the end of the month of *July* nothing else was wanting but to make the slides upon which the vessel was to be launched into the water. These were 25 fathoms long; for the vessel could not be put on the stocks quite near the sea, on account of the tide flowing pretty high. On the 10th of *August* she was launched, and named after the packet-boat, *St Peter*, out of the wrecks of which this vessel was built. She might be called a single masted hucker; for according

ing to her tackle she approached nearest to this sort of vessels. A quantity of cannon-balls, cartridges, and all the iron-work that remained of the former vessel, they made serve as ballast. The mast was got in, ropes, sails, and rudder properly disposed. Happily it was just a calm, without which they would hardly have succeeded. The ship lay from N. N. W. to N. E. exposed to the open sea. If a storm had arisen she might easily have been stranded again on the coast. She drew five feet water, and could have carried a greater burthen, but this was sufficient for the intended purpose.

The crew being embarked, they put to sea on the 10th of *August* towards the evening. The boat belonging to the former ship was taken in tow, only by way of trying whether they could preserve her; if it was not practicable, they resolved to set her adrift. They passed by the rocks and other shallow places that evening, and found from four to nine fathoms water; after which they took to their oars. When by means of these they were advanced about four leagues from the shore, a gentle breeze from the north began to spring up, with which they proceeded on their voyage. It is surprising how well the vessel sailed and work'd. Had she been built by an experienced master, she could not have well sailed better. The next day at noon they were in sight of the south-east point of *Bering*'s island, at a distance of four leagues N. by E. to which they gave the name of *Cape Manati*, from the above-mentioned sea-cows, which herd more here than in any other parts. The north latitude of this cape is 54 deg. 55 min. or about 55 deg. whereas the place where they resided this winter had been observed to be almost in 56 deg. On the 18th of *August* in the morning they had a strong contrary wind from south-west; wherefore it was resolved to cut the tow rope, and set the boat adrift, for fear the burthen of it might be hurtful to the vessel. On the same day about noon the vessel began to be very leaky; two pumps were not sufficient to keep her free, they were obliged to use water buckets, and throw overboard their heavy goods, in order to lighten the vessel, to discover the leak, which they found out and stopped so well that they made use of but one pump, and that not constantly. On the 25th of *August* they came in sight of the land of *Kamtschatka*; the following day they were so happy as to make the bay of *Awatscha*, and on the 27th they entered the harbour of St *Peter* and *Paul*. What exultations this must have

caused

caused in our sailors, every one may easily conceive. All distress and danger to which they had been exposed, was now over. They came to a plenteous magazine of provisions, which Captain *Tschirikow* had left there. They wintered here in commodious dwellings, having first attempted to return to *Ochotzk* in the same autumn, but were prevented by contrary and violent winds. In the mean time the vessel was clean'd and put in a condition for another voyage, they set sail again in the month of *May* following, to carry back to *Ochotzk* the whole ship's company. *Waxel* went from the harbour of *Peter* and *Paul* to *Jakutzk*, and having wintered there, proceeded to *Jeniseisk*, where, on his arrival in *October*, 1744, he found Captain *Tschirikow*, who had received orders from the senate to take up his residence there, till a resolution should be taken with respect to the continuing or not the *Kamtschatka* navigations. *Waxel* stayed at *Jeniseisk*, and when *Tschirikow*, was ordered in 1745 to *Petersburg*, *Waxel* took upon him the command of the mariners there, and did not arrive with them at *Petersburg* till *January* 1749, which time may be fixed as the end of the second *Kamtschatka* expedition, so that it lasted near 16 years.

As to the academical company of travellers, *Gmelin* and I arrived at *Petersburg* on *Feb.* 15, 1743, having passed through all the parts of *Siberia*. But *Steller*, who stayed in *Kamtschatha* after *Waxel*, to make researches in natural history, did not enjoy this good luck. He immerged himself without necessity, though with a good intention, in matters that did not belong to his department; for which he was called to an account by the provincial chancery at *Jakutzk*. *Steller* vindicated himself so perfectly, that the Vice Governor there gave him permission to proceed on his journey, the proceedings were not sent to the Senate at *Petersburg* so soon as transacted. The Senate, who had intelligence of his passing through *Tobolsk*, sent an express to meet him, and to carry him back to *Jakutzk*. And soon after advice being received from *Irkutzk*, of his acquital, another express was dispatched to annul the first order. In the mean time, the first express met *Steller* at *Solikamsk*, and had carried him back as far as *Tara*, before the second express overtook him. He then proceeded without delay, on his return for *Petersburg* by the way of *Tobolsk*, but got no farther than *Tumen*, where he died of a fever in *November* 1746, in company of one *Hau* a surgeon, who had been with him in the *Kamtschatka* expedition. I have thought it necessary to relate

(66)

relate these circumstances, because many falsities have been propagated abroad concerning him, nay, even his death has been doubted. He was born on the 10th of *March* 1709, at *Winsheim* in *Franconia*. His industry and ingenuity would have been of much greater use to the learned world had it pleased divine providence to prolong his life. *Gmelin* returned, in the year 1747, to *Tubingen*, his native place, where he died professor of botany and chymistry, on the 20th of *May* 1755. The loss of him is likewise not inconsiderable to the republic of the learned; since he had not, by far, finished transcribing the many observations collected by him in *Siberia*. Since that time nothing farther has been attempted in those seas, by especial order from the Empress; but some private persons have made several trips to *Berings* and the neighbouring isles. The catching of Beavers in those parts has enticed people to them, and they never returned without great quantities which always produced large profits. This has brought considerable revenues to the crown, by paying a tenth as toll; wherefore the governors at *Jakutzk*, *Ochotzk*, and in *Kamtschatka*, have encouraged the merchants and *Promyschleni*, to carry on the trade; the small hucker *Peter* being left for the use of these people to whom the vessel was of great service. Indeed, it must be a vessel like this, or rather less, in which the islands situated in those parts, are to be approached, and the landing place must be free from rocks; the most proper would be a sandy coast, that the vessel might with the flood run towards the land and remain dry at low water, where she would be safe from danger. Such places are said to have been found only on the west side of *Berings* island, nor is there any harbour, or bay, round about the whole island, where a vessel may lie at anchor, without fear of being dashed by violent winds to pieces against the rocks, or else stranded.

In 1753, a letter was published at *Berlin*, entitled, *Lettre d'un Officier de la Marine Russienne à un Seigneur de la Court*, taking notice of a map published by M. *de Lisle* at *Paris*, in the year 1752, representing not only the discoveries of the *Kamtschatka* expedition, but even those ascribed to Admiral *de Fonte* with a printed explanation; the author of the Letter found that M. *de Lisle* had very indifferent materials for composing his map. He discovered in it, and in the explanation, several errors and untruths, and observed in what a groundless manner the author would appropriate to himself, and to his brother M. *de Lisle de la Croyere*, who died in *Kamtschatka*,

the

the honour of thefe difcoveries. All this he fhewed candidly. The Letter was firft printed fingly; and afterwards corrected and inferted in the 18th Vol. of *Nouvelle Bibliotheque Germanique.* At *London* an *Englifh* tranflation of it was publifhed, with fome obfervations by Mr *Arthur Dobbs*, the great promoter of the Northern navigation. The annexed map of the new *Kamtfchatka* difcoveries, lately publifhed by the Academy of Sciences, was made under my infpection. Some of the firft copies have the date 1754, for the map was finifhed and engraved that year. But I have revifed and corrected it in feveral places, and changed the date to 1758, in which particulars the fubfequent copies differ from the former. The memoir mentioned in the original title is *no* other than this treatife to begin on the weft fide.

Siberia is copied from a new map of *Siberia*, which is done by my order, according to the obfervations and defcriptions made by me in that country, but is not yet engraved. A very great difference will be obferved between this and the maps of *Siberia* in the *Ruffian* Atlas.

The coafts of the frozen fea are drawn according to the above defcribed navigations.

To the *Tfchukotfkoi Nos*, I have given a new form, it is a narrow Ifthmus, which has been more than once croffed on foot from the fea of *Kolyma*, to the fea of *Anadir*. And I think this *Nos* muft extend a great way farther beyond the Ifthmus. I am afraid it is reprefented too fmall yet, for which reafon the out-line is only marked with points, to fhew the uncertainty. I might have put Iflands about the *Tfchukotfkoi Nos*, if the intelligencies received of them were of authority enough to determine their fituation. As for the Ifland *Puchotfkoi*, which is found in the maps publifhed in *Holland*, after the death of *Peter* the Great, and in that of *Strahlenberg*, the name is quite unknown in *Siberia* unlefs, inftead of this, it be called *Tfchukotfkoi*.

Anadirfkoi Oftrog, and the courfe of the river *Anadir*, are placed more northerly in this than in the former maps. By following the obfervations made at *Anadirfkoi Oftrog*, which is in 66 deg. 9 min. and according to this alfo, the fituation of the *Penfchfkin* Bay is regulated. For the diftance between *Anadirfkoi Oftrog*, and the mouth of the river *Penfkina*, has been found, to be not much above 200 Werfts. And befides it was neceffary that the *Penfkinfkian* Bay
should

should extend farther towards the North than in the former maps, on account of the many confiderable rivers that empty themfelves into it, of which only the principal ones can be pointed out. Thefe coafts were never before properly defcribed. It may reafonably be reckoned a fault in both the *Kamtfchatka* expeditions, not to have taken notice of fuch occurrences as thefe.

An error has alfo been committed in this map, in determining the fituation of *Ochotzk*, which proceeded from my not having received the aftronomical obfervations from *Ochotzk*. But I thought, that according to the menfuration and defcription of the roads from *Jakutz* to *Ochotzk*, the diftance between both places, as it is fet down in the *Ruffian* Atlas, was two degrees too much in longitude: Confequently I placed *Ochotzk* two degrees more to the Weftward. After this I received the obfervations of the true longitude of *Ochotzk*, which is 160 deg. 59 min. 15 fec. Its latitude 59 deg. 20 min. Any difagreement with this, is to be attributed to the following too precifely my firft map, and becaufe this determination is not made ufe of.

Concerning the coaft between *Ochotzk* and the river *Amur*, it muft run not towards the South, as in all maps publifhed hitherto it does, but from *Ochotzk*, as far as the river *Ud*, towards the South Weft, and from the river *Ud*, as far as the *Amur*, to the South Eaft; and in this manner their coaft is reprefented in the prefent map. At *Udfkoi Oftrog*, obfervations have been made of the Lat. It has been found at one time 55 deg. 10 min. and at another 55 deg. 27. min. whence a medium of 55 deg. 18 min. is to be concluded on; the reafon for reprefenting the coaft in thofe parts in the aforefaid manner is, that it agrees better with the meafured and geometrical diftance defcribed between *Jakutzk* and *Udfkoi Oftrog*, and the multitude of rivers that fall into the fea, between *Ochotzk* and *Udfkoi Oftrog*, and with their diftances communicated by perfons acquainted with thofe parts: For, if the coaft from *Ochotzk* runs South Weft, then the rivers will have more room, and the diftance between them be more agreeable to truth.

With refpect to the *Shantarian* Iflands they are only in a manner hinted at, in the map, without making the fituation agree with my defcription of them, which, though drawn as carefully as poffible, will hardly correfpond with the truth. For whofoever navigates with attention in this fea hereafter, will doubtlefs find the fituation, magnitude,

nitude, and number of the Iſlands quite different. The Iſland ſituate oppoſite the mouth of the river *Amur*, as well as all the coaſts and countries, belonging to *China*, being taken from *Du Halde*'s maps, will require no great vindication for miſtakes made in them. But that the *Chineſe* maps of thoſe parts are not free from errors, may be ſuppoſed, becauſe no *Jeſuit* ever was there, and the Mandarines ſent by *Chan Cang-hi* to deſcribe the Iſland, took but little pains about it. Many other diſcoveries might be made there, if a voyage was undertaken for that purpoſe. The many various opinions of geographers about the land of *Jeſo*, or rather Iſland, that it is ſituated in the middle between *Kamtſchatka* and *Japan* do not clear up any thing ſatisfactory from the antient diſcoveries, ſince ſome connected this country with *Japan*, others with *America*, or with Eaſt *Tartary*, and by others *Kamtſchatka* was taken for it; then again they made one, and at another time ſeveral Iſlands of it. Great credit is given to the account of the ſhip *Caſtricom*, publiſhed in the collection of *Thevenot*, in the third Tom. of Voyages *au Nord*, in father *Charlevoix*'s *Hiſtoire du Japon*. (Tom. 2. p. 494) but I cannot perſuade myſelf to take it with M. *Buache*, for deciſive. There is too little of a proper ſea journal in it, and nothing from which one might conclude that the captain of the ſhip has taken pains to get an exact knowledge of the land he has ſeen, or the ſea in which he ſailed. No computation of the longitude is obſerved, and yet it is not to be believed that the maſter had been neglectful in this reſpect. The courſe of the ſhip *Caſtricom*, was moſtly towards the North, and hence moſt maps repreſent *Jeſo* nearly under the ſame meridian with the North coaſt of *Japan*, which is an error that Mr *D'Anville* alone, has, in ſome meaſure, corrected in his map of *Aſia*. The account of the ſhip *Breſkes*, which ſailed out at the ſame time with the *Caſtricom*, on the diſcovery of *Jeſo*, contains much exacter obſervations; but they are little known, and therefore have not yet been made uſe of by any geographer; for though it ſeems, as if M. *D'Anville* had known ſomething of them, ſince the ſituation he has given the land of *Jeſo*, comes neareſt to that given in the relation of the ſhip *Breſkes*; yet, from other circumſtances, the contrary may be ſuppoſed. M. *D'Anville* truſts much to probabilities; theſe have cauſed him to take *Jeſo*, *Staten* Iſland, and *Companys* Iſland, with the *Jeſoian* Iſlands, from *Japan*, to the Iſland *Nadeſchdas*, for one. They have likewiſe perhaps miſled him to connect ſeveral

places

places from the relation of the *Caſtricom*; for inſtance, *Blydenburg*, *Tamari Aniwa*, Cape *Aniwa*, &c. with Eaſt *Tartary*, and to place Cape *Patience*, which is generally eſteemed to be the North point of the Iſland *Jeſo*, on the South point of the Iſland of *Sachalin Ula*; in which, whether he is right or wrong cannot eaſily be decided. What information the account of the ſhip *Breſkes*, from *Witzen* affords, I will inſert becauſe it is rare: This ſhip in 1643, ſet ſail in company with the *Caſtricom*, for the diſcovery of *Tartary*, and was ſeparated by a ſtorm from the latter, on the Eaſt coaſt of *Japan*, and diſcovered the land of *Jeſo*. In the month of *June* ſhe ſailed through the Streights, which ſeparate the land of *Jeſo* from *Japan*. In 41 deg. 50 min. North lat. and in 164 deg. 48 min. long. On the point of land, which was firſt diſcovered, appeared eight or ten rocks like ſails, and from theſe a great ridge extended a mile into the ſea. They ſaw there ſmall veſſels (Prawen) the rowers had in each hand an oar, which they uſed alternately, ſtriking into the water and went very ſwift, they appeared to be a ſenſible people, had black long rough beards, and were of a tawny complexion; on the fore part of their heads, about the breadth of three fingers they wore long hair, which toward the hind part was cut off. It was remarked that, in token of gratitude, they folded their hands together over their heads, they were clothed in Bear-ſkins; their weapons were bows and arrows. From thence the ſhip ſailed much to the Eaſtward, and the ſailors caught plenty of cod. In 43 deg. 4 min. North lat. they ſaw land again; in 44 deg. 4 min. lat. veſſels came to the ſhip, whoſe people were ſtrong of body, and ſenſible in converſation; they had women with them of a brown complexion, and their lips and hands painted blue. Theſe wore their hair round about their heads cut off about three fingers breadth below their ears, and had an aſpect like young men. They took much delight in drinking of brandy; ſome of theſe people alſo wore cloaths after the *Japanneſe* faſhion; others had croſſes on their coats. Beſides bows and arrows, they were armed with ſabres, (howers) alſo which are made like thoſe in *Japan*; the hilts of their ſwords were ornamented with ſmall pieces of gold, the blades with ſilver backs, and the ſheaths with foliage. The belts of their ſabres were embroidered with gold, they wore ſilver rings and *Nuremburg* beads in their ears; ſeals and beaver ſkins, and ſome *Indian* ſtuffs, were ſeen among them; their veſſels were made of hollowed trees. In 43 deg. 45 min. North lat. land was again diſcovered,

(71)

covered, as also in 44 deg. 12 min. lat. and 167 deg. 21 min. long. They saw high land, and perceived many Islands, and the main land. A little more northerly many seals were observed, and a sort of grass floating in the sea. In 45 deg. 12 min. North lat. and 169 deg. 36 min. long. the land appeared afar off like Islands; but when they came near it, they found it was a continent covered with snow in many places; here they went on shore, but the country was desert. In a valley, not far from the coast, there was a brook of clear fresh water, along which they found also low shrubs, cherry-trees, sorrel, wild cabbage, leeks and nettles; they saw neither men nor beasts, except one fox. In 46 deg. 15 min. lat. and 172 deg. 16 min. long. as also in 172 deg. 53 min. long. appeared a chain of high mountains. Land was likewise discovered in 47 deg. 8 min. lat. and 173 deg. 53 min. long. but no foot set on it. This land lies, according to the journal of the ship *Breskes*, 12 deg. more Easterly than the East point of *Japon*, which is situate in 38 deg. 4 min. difference of lat. 9 deg. 38 min. course N. E. by E. and S. W. by W.

From whence I conclude that the situation of the pretended land of *Jeso* is the same with the Islands laid down in this map, and that the latter may without any inconsistency be put in the place of the former. For neither the navigation of the *Breskes*, or of the *Castricom*, prove that all the land these ships met with was united, *Matsmey* is taken for one Island by Mess. *de Lisle* and *Buache* notwithstanding many accounts, especially those of the Missionaries of *Japon*, and even those of the *Castricom* are against this opinion. But as submission is already paid in this point, why is not the same acknowledgement made in regard to the Islands *Kunaschir*, *Urup Figurnoi*, *Zitornoi*, &c.

The reality of the Island of *Nedescha* is not denied; but if the journals of the *Castricom* and the *Breskes* have any credit, and all the land which they have seen, is taken for continent, then this also cannot stand. Which, if we grant them the said navigation, proves too much, and consequently is not at all conclusive, even for Mess. *D'Lisle* and *Buache*. Neither is it a proof for them, that the *Europeans* in *Japon* have heard the land of *Jeso* described as a large continent. What has been said above, that the inhabitants of all these Islands are called by the *Japannese* by one common name of *Jeso* may have occasioned the mistake; with which, the ships *Castricom* and *Breskes* being prejudiced, they believed therefore that all the land they saw, was one and the same island. By this they may have been prevented

vented from making enquiries into the openings and bays observed by them, which were probably Streights between the Islands. Thus it is even unnecessary to call to our assistance a forced change of places, as has been done above, for the explanation of the present situation of those parts. *Van Keulen* sets down in his map, that *Jeso* is contiguous to *Tartary*, of which hitherto nothing can be said with certainty; though I am sure enough that *Jeso* is divided into Islands. Such like testimonies serve at least to secure an opinion from being called rashness. The same order and names of the Island have been retained as they are set down in the *Russian* Atlas, according to Capt. *Spangberg*'s voyage, without employing any other assistance. The comparing of these accounts with the former may be of use in future enquiries into these parts, which it is to be wish'd will not be left undone, in order to remove all doubt that may remain concerning the land of *Jeso*. *Japon* is laid out in imitation of Mess. *D'Anville*, and *Bellin*. It is true father *Charlevoix* says, that according to a new map corrected after the astronomical observations of the *Jesuits* in *China*, this empire lies between 157 and 175 deg. long. But this is an evident error, from whence it would follow that, contrary to experience, ships would be obliged to sail from *Kamtschatka*, to *Japon* directly Southward. My emendations in respect to *Kamtschatka*, may be seen by comparing this map with the former. In general, *Kamtschatka* appears now, a good deal longer than before, since the *Penschinskian* bay takes up a greater extent to the North. The River *Peschina* emptied itself, in the *Kirilowian* map on the West, and on the map in the *Russian* Atlas on the East side into the bay: Here it falls into the Northermost corner of it. All the rivers have almost got another situation, and many of them a corrected orthography too. The most remarkable mistakes were in the rivers *Plutora* and *Tigil* or *Kigil*, the first of which was laid out two degrees too far to the South, and the second so much too far Northerly. There remained not so much as one degree of lat. between the mouths of both; and the difference ought to amount to five degrees. There is no room left here for uncertainty or doubt, as these rivers belong to the principal ones of the country; and they are frequently visited by the inhabitants of both the *Russian Ostrogs*, on the river *Kamtschatka*; since the road from the river *Penschina* to the *Tigil*, and from thence to the rivers *Kamtschatka*, *Bolschaia reka*, &c. has been described by surveyors; and since, lastly, it is exactly

actly known in *Kamtschatka* that the rivers which fall into the sea on either sides, are opposite to one another. People travel from *Anadriskoi Ostrog*, to the river *Kamtschatka*, and pass the river *Olura* half way: consequently it must be in about 61 deg. North lat. for the mouth of the river *Kamtschatka* is in 56 deg. or something more Northerly. But the mouth of the *Tigil* it is known for certain to be in the same lat. with the mouth of *Kamtschatka*. At *Bolcheretskoi Ostrog*, and in St. *Peter* and *Paul*'s harbour, astronomical observations have been made, which determined the situation of these places,

	Latitude.	Longitude.
Bolscheretskoi Ostrog in	52 54½	174 10
St Peter and *Paul*'s harbour	53 1¼	176 12½
Mouth of the *Bolschaia-reka*	52 54	
South point of *Kamtschatka*	51 3	

This may suffice at present concerning *Kamtschatka*. As to that part of the map which exhibits the *American* discoveries, they are taken from drawings made on board the ships, after the best reconciliation of the different accounts, and therefore I am not answerable for it, if, in some places, a difference should be observed between the description and the map. My work herein has been no more than to connect together, according to probability, by points, the coasts that had been seen in various places. Monf. *Buache*, who before had taken the coast seen between 51 and 52 deg. North lat. and 21 deg. long. from *Awatscha* (Mr *de Lisle* says mistakenly 12 deg.) for a distinct and separate country or island, has followed this advice in his newest maps; and in general has hit the mark pretty well, notwithstanding several coasts belonging to the connexion, were not known to him. But since here the case may be the same that caused us to say so much on occasion of *Jeso*, I mean, an uncertainty whether the land be island or continent, prudence requires us not to trust too much to supposition, but to leave future discovery to confirm which of these is the real circumstance in this affair.

I have likewise thought proper to connect the *Russian* discoveries, after the example of Mess. *de Lisle* and *Buache*, with the parts of *America* already known. For this purpose it was necessary to be

L directed

directed by a map of *America*, the exactness of which cannot be denied. I chose that of Mr *Greens*, it being just at hand during the work. According to which, therein, the then known parts of *America* are planned. Had such astronomical observations been taken on board of our ships, as were designed, the distance between the new discovered parts, and those already known before, might have been determined with more certainty. But for want of that our sole and only grounds are the ship's reckoning; which we shall not insist upon, supposing future navigations should shew a difference from the present determination. Till that shall happen, the decision of Mr *Dobbs*'s, doubt may be deferred, he will not take all for continent that our people have seen, except it be confirmed by new discoveries. All is to represent a large island. Indeed, the hoped for North West passage from *Hudson*'s Bay to the *South Sea*, is rendered more difficult by our opinion, and looses almost its probability. But I have given the grounds, why one may reasonably suppose that the continent of *America* extends as far as the neighbourhood of the country of *Tschuktschi*. I could wish Mr *Dobbs* might be right, *Russia* would lose nothing by it. Her future possessions would be the more incontestible, since no *European* would be able to boast of having ever had knowledge of this great island. And, on the other hand, the enterprizes of the *English*, with respect to finding out the North West passage, which certainly is to be wished, for more reasons than one, might be the more conveniently supported. But it seems to me, that hitherto the contrary opinion is the most probable. What has been said above, is a sufficient declaration why the Western sea of Mr *William de Lisle*, and the pretended discoveries of admiral *de Fonte*, have no place here. It is always better to leave a void space for future discoveries, than to fill it with such uncertainties; a new navigation is requisite to evince the truth, or falsity of this matter. Finally if my readers find nothing neither in the map, nor in this description of the pertinent account of Mr *De Guigne*, which he has collected from *Chinese* writings, and in 1752 communicated to the *Paris* Academy of *Belles Lettres*, and likewise inserted in the Journal *des Scavans*, for the month of *December*, of the same year, the judgment of a greater connoisseur in the *Chinese* language, and History, than myself, *viz.* That if the famous father *Gaubil*, at *Pekin*, will excuse me. The ability and sincerity of this man cannot be questioned. He has given proofs

thereof

thereof in many writings, which do honour to his country, his order, and our academy, of which he is a member. M. *de Guigne*, has to do with a countryman, a man whose assiduous endeavours deserve much praise. His judgment, therefore must be founded on an entire conviction. But it so little favours M *De Guigne's* account, as rather to declare them to be empty fables. The love of truth, and my own justification obliges me to add father *Gaubill's* own words, from a letter of the 23d of *November* 1755, to the illustrious president of our Academy. They are, *Nous avons vu ici les Cartes de Mess. de Lisle et Buache, sur les decouvertes des Russien en Amerique. Un François, nommé Monsf. de Guignes, qui etudié la Chinose à Paris, croit qu'il a decouvert dans les libres Chinois un Voyage des Chinois de la Chine jusqu' à la Californie en Amerique, dans l'an de J. C. 458. Il a fait graver une Carte de ce Voyage, et a lu la dessus divers Memoirs à l'Academie des Inscriptions et Belles Lettres. Je crois qui ce voyage est une fable, et j'ai ecrit à Mr de Guignes mes raisons en repondant à une de ses Lettres ou il me detailloit sa decouverte.*

" We have seen here the maps of Mess. *de Lisle* and *Buache*, on the discoveries of the *Russians* in *America*. A *Frenchman* named M. *De Guigne*, who studies the *Chinese* at *Paris*, believes he has discovered in the *Chinese* books, a voyage of the *Chinese* from *China*, as far as *California*, in *America*, in the year of *Jesus Christ* 458. He has had a map engraved of this voyage, and has read upon it divers memoirs to the academy of inscriptions and *Belles Lettres*. I believe that this voyage is a fable, and I have wrote to M. *De Guigne's* himself, my reasons, in answering one of his letters, where he gave me a detail of his discovery." Now, it is M. *De Guigne's* business to communicate to the world his grounds for supporting his opinion against father *Gaubil*. I beg leave to conclude with a general observation. We see that the result of all is, that although much has been done, yet something still remains to be executed. May we not hope to bring to its perfection such an important work? *Russia's* glorious sovereigns place, in imitation of *Peter* the Great, their highest honour in promoting the sciences. They endeavour not only to make them known more and more among their own subjects; but they also communicate to other nations, what by their regulations, and, at their own expences, they do for the extending of the sciences. No praise is more lasting than this. By which a prince erects for himself monuments, that no time can deface, no accidents destroy. Such a monument does the first *Kamtschatka* expedition raise for its author *Peter the Great*. Such glory does the second expedition give to the happy reign of *Elizabeth*, our great Empress.

This account of the discoveries already made, are published by her order, for the use of the whole world; and the hopes of bringing them to perfection.

F I N I S.

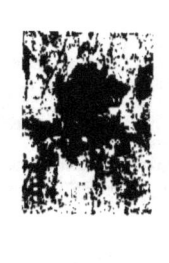

A MAP
of the
DISCOVERIES made by the RUSSIANS
on the
North West Coast of AMERICA.
Published by the Royal Academy of Sciences at Petersburg.
LONDON
Republished by Thomas Jefferys Geographer
to his MAJESTY.

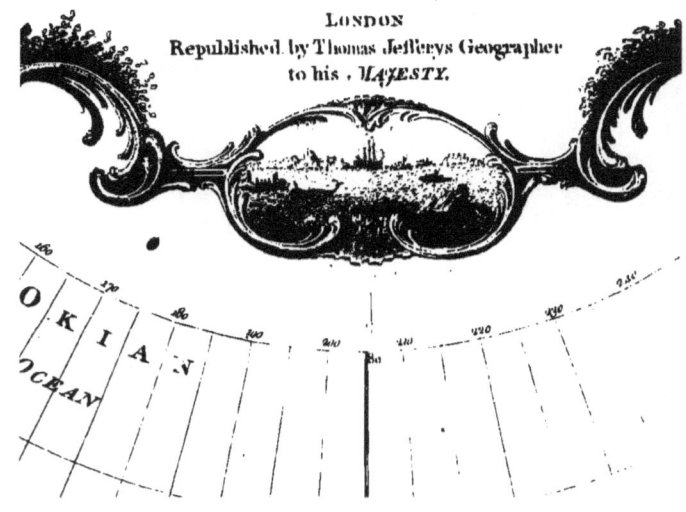

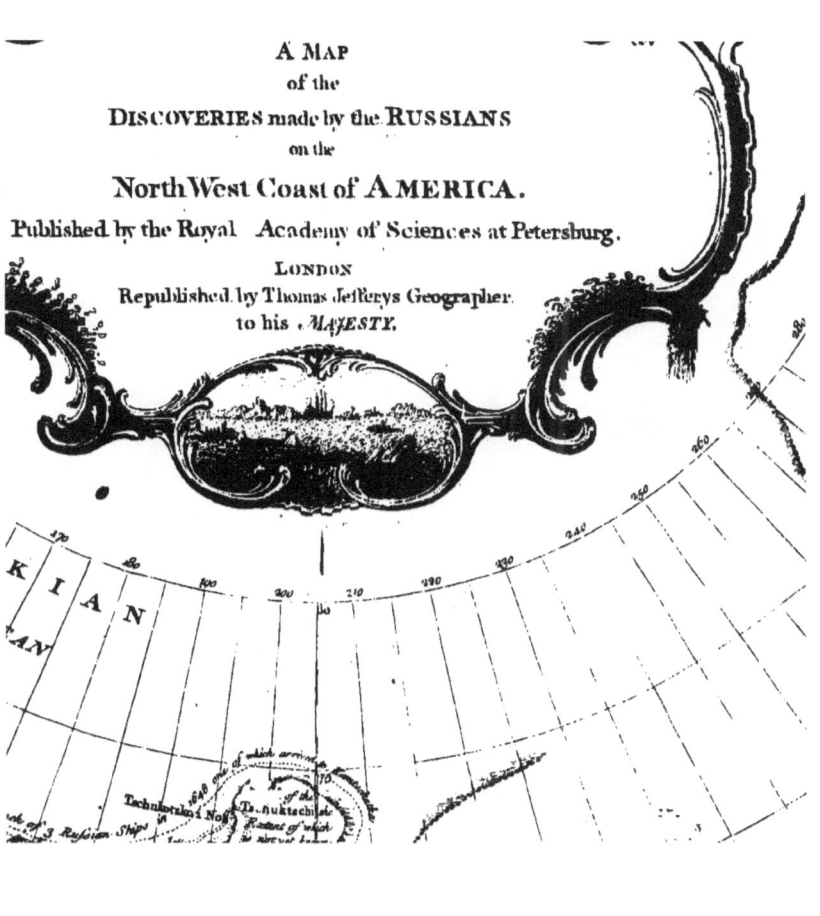

A OR PAC

www.ingramcontent.com/pod-product-compliance
Lightning Source LLC
Chambersburg PA
CBHW030358170426
43202CB00010B/1412